A Woman's Path to the Heart of Islam

A Woman's Path to the Heart of Islam

Interviews by Rachel and Jean-Pierre
Cartier with Eva de Vitray-Meyerovitch

An English translation of *Islam, l'autre visage.*
Albin Michel: Espaces libres, Paris 1995,
first published by Criterion, 1991

Translated by Cathryn Goddard

FONS VITAE

First published in 2020 by
Fons Vitae
49 Mockingbird Valley Drive
Louisville, KY 40207
http://www.fonsvitae.com
Email: fonsvitaeky@aol.com

Library of Congress Control Number: 2020944395
ISBN 978-1887752-220

Printed in Canada

With heartfelt thanks to the editor Katharine Branning
and to the proofreader Anne Ogden.

Contents

Preface
by Sheikh Khaled Bentounes

Eva de Vitray-Meyerovitch was a person absorbed by the inner quest for reality. What moves us to try to see beyond illusion and make such a challenging voyage? In the external world, suffering, along with our own painful rejection of self, can fuel our passion to discover the Divine within. Positive attraction also spurs our search, as we are drawn magnetically by truth, beauty and unconditional love. This slim yet profound book tells the story of Eva's journey, and reflects many of our own inner yearnings, in the open sphere of spirituality, beyond the confines of culture and our own defensiveness.

In the early 1950s a college classmate of Eva's returned to France from Pakistan and brought her a gift: the writings of Mohammed Iqbal. She was like a flower waiting to bloom, with a keen mind already well formed by years studying law and philosophy. The book spoke frequently of Jalaluddin Rumi, one of the world's great mystical poets. His prose combined lucidity and ecstasy, touching the heart of this intellectual with a husband and two sons. She threw herself into translating the book from English into French, and then plunged into studying Persian in order to devote her life to the works of Rumi.

Perhaps we each have to go beyond ourselves to find ourselves. Our own context becomes routine and associated with social and cultural baggage. We may be able to see more clearly in new surroundings that give us a fresh perspective on ourselves, even when facing the limitations of a less well known language or environment. Eva was drawn by the mysterious Orient to a new dimension. For more than a decade, her work consisted of translating, studying and teaching others about the writings of two Muslim masters of the meaning of life, Rumi and Iqbal.

She could easily have remained what she already was, a Roman Catholic scholar of Islamic mysticism. Her world, however, was being rocked by the Algerian struggle for independence. A minority of European colonizers denied the nationality of the over-whelmingly Muslim population, claiming Algiers was an integral part of France. Pope John XXIII himself pleaded for the Algerians' right to self-determination.

Eva chose the difficult path, siding with a civilization many of her compatriots considered inferior. This human judgment, pitting civilizations – each with unique qualities and contributions – against each other, really reflects our ego's need to feel superior. She stood up for what she felt mattered, freely choosing what she knew to be a far more demanding journey. She did not reject Judaism or Christianity, the roots of her own cultural frame of reference, but chose what she felt was the path that encompassed both traditions, Islam.

And how indeed could she reject a religion, when the Qur'an itself so clearly states, "Those who believe – those who are Jews, Christians and Sabaeans, *whosoever* believes in God and the Last Day, and acts righteously shall have their reward with their Lord . . ." (Qur'an 2:62).

We each find the spiritual traditions that nurture us with useful practices, provide us with a sense of community, and give expression to our innermost being. Usually we find them within a single religion, occasionally we draw from many religions and sometimes we move outside all of them.

The Qur'an reminds us, "Say, we believe in God and the revelation given to us and to Abraham, Ismail, Isaac, Jacob and the tribes, and given to Moses and Jesus and (all) prophets from their Lord. We make no distinction between any of them, and unto God do we surrender" (Qur'an 2:136).

Remarkably, this powerful affirmation is cited five times in the holy book of Islam. Like the reminders of a loving parent who knows the foibles of children, this repetition seems to reflect divine awareness of our human proclivity to claim that our particular messengers bring the only expression of Truth. (Reference to Qur'an 2:136, 2:285, 3:84, 4:150, 4:152. These last two citations include the paired divine judgments that, on the one hand, those who deny any messengers of God are disbelievers and, on the other hand, that those who acknowledge all messengers of God will assuredly be duly rewarded.)

The very word "messengers" in Arabic means "those sent by." Are we not all, each in our own way, sent by the Almighty? An oft cited saying of the Prophet Mohammed tells us to "Seek knowledge, even in China." In the 7th century, he acknowledged both the wisdom (the Arabic word used, *'ilm*, includes science, know-how and spiritual knowledge) of the rich non-Abrahamic traditions and the interconnectedness of our world.

Eva was well aware of the broad metaphorical interpretation of the Qur'an that moves beyond literal meanings and historical contexts. The latter can cause sacred writings to appear contradictory to the uninitiated. Inspiring texts can guide us in our lives, but should not be used to divide us, as they are necessarily both captured in a moment in time and broader in scope than many readers can fathom.

By her conversion, Eva paid the price of rejection within her own society, by many friends, colleagues and family. She also had to deal with qualified acceptance by the community she chose to embrace, by those (present in all religions) who treat the convert as lesser in stature, knowledge and authenticity. Moved by tenacious enthusiasm (*en + theos*, Greek, "inspired by the divine") for the beauty of Rumi's work, she produced dozens of books and articles that are our shared heritage today.

Her life is a testimony to her profound belief in the sense of the kinship of all creation. Earlier she had become a Muslim and performed the Haj pilgrimage. In Cairo she sat at the feet of Sheikh Hafiz Tijani and asked him to be her master. As he placed his robe tenderly around her shoulders, he said, "Were I to accept you as my disciple, I would give you many things to recite daily which would be too much for you, and I would not want you to feel guilty."

Years later, she was received as a disciple of the Moroccan Sufi Sheikh Hamza Boutchichi. She drank like a sponge from his well of truth. Her compassion and wisdom increased through her years of experience and practice with Sufi masters, complementing her understanding of Rumi, her ultimate spiritual guide. She, like Rumi, found her true community with people of all faiths, in principles that link us, not in dogmas that can divide.

She sought the universal connection that goes beyond formal religion, in the compassionate message of the Prophet Mohammed, as expressed in the Qur'an: "O people! We created you from male and female, and have made you into nations and tribes that you may know one another (with the connotation of *learn from one another*). The noblest among you in the sight of God is the best in conduct, and God is the All Knowing One." (Qur'an 49:13)

Rumi invites us to look beyond superficial divisions of culture, language, nationality and religion, without allowing them to be barriers to our understanding, so we can rejoice together in our essential unity: His writings bring heart and mind together with this notion, as seen in this example:

> If ten lamps are gathered in the same place,
>   each differs from the other only in form.
>
> When you turn your face toward the lamps,
>   you can't really distinguish their separate lights . . .
>
> In spiritual matters, there is neither division, nor number;
>   in spiritual matters, there is neither separation
>   nor individuals.
>
> Sweet is the unity of the Friend with friends;
>   connect in the spiritual sense: form is but a rebel.
>
> Let it be struck down to discover unity's hidden treasure
>   beneath the surface.

> *Mathnawi,* I: 680-686;
> from Eva's French translation
> from the Persian, page 93.

Her path, a woman's journey to the heart, reflects the epic hero's voyage to distant lands with exotic tongues, facing challenges from within and from without. She was inspired and guided by people of years gone by, as well as those present in her own generation, in addition to the traditions and symbols that illuminate the way for us all.

From her struggles, she brought back to us gifts of insight, treasures from the East, for a world in sore need of mutual respect and understanding. Her life of surrender to a higher purpose is a testimony of determination to transcend the fear of that which is different, in order to discover the encompassing love that connects us in all our rich diversity.

> Sheikh Khaled Bentounes
> Paris, France

Introduction
by Rachel and Jean-Pierre Cartier

When we [Rachel and Jean-Pierre Cartier] first entered Eva de Vitray-Meyerovitch's office to begin these interviews, we immediately noticed a large bound book in plain view in the middle of her desk, a book that makes you want to caress its binding for a while before diving into it.

"It arrived this morning," she told us. Beneath her neutral tone, we caught a glimmer of a certain pride. Well-deserved pride, for this was a work to which she had consecrated all her strength and all her talent for more than ten years: the *Mathnawi* of Jalaluddin Rumi.[1] The text represents fifty thousand verses never before translated into French and of singular beauty, an immense song of love, the heart-to-heart dialogue between one of the world's purest mystics and his Divine Master. More than a book, the work is a veritable runway for take-off, which Rumi himself suggests in saying: "I did not recite the *Mathnawi* for people to carry it around or recite it, but for them to put this book under their feet and fly with it."

For several years now, uncanny circumstances seemed to link our paths to Eva de Vitray-Meyerovitch. Both Rachel and I readily saw an act of Providence in this wondrous coincidence. We met her in the home of Sheikh Bentounes when we were writing *The Prophets of Today*, which gave us the idea of immersing ourselves, with great enthusiasm, in her works and discovering through them the literary treasures of Muslim mysticism. This discovery, even today, is a source of joy for us.

Naturally, when we wrote *Femmes de Lumière (Enlightened Women)*, we wanted to ask Eva de Vitray-Meyerovitch what she thought about the theme of our book. And once again, the interview we had with her whetted our appetite. We discovered in this

---

1. Jalaluddin Rumi (1207-1273). Sufi mystic, scholar, and poet born in present-day Afghanistan and died in Konya, Turkey.

intellectual woman such a strong heart-connection connection, such fervor in the quest, such a love for Muslim mystics, and, even more obviously, for her beloved Rumi, that, slowly but surely, the idea of this book came to us.

The 1991 Gulf War was just beginning its military phase. The very air we breathed was charged with fear and malaise, as well as a strange warlike exaltation in certain quarters. Rachel and I were aghast to sense the rising tide around us of suspicion and hatred towards Islam. The tension we experienced at that time encouraged oversimplifications and dubious combinations of ideas. Even from some of our friends we heard lines of reasoning that startled us: "You are really too naive. In your last two books, you talked with people who presented Islam as a religion of tolerance and pure mysticism. Open your eyes: the real Islam, the one you don't want to see, is that of the ayatollahs or Saddam Hussein, the Islam of hatred, of holy war; a constant threat that we have to combat if we don't want to be devoured by it."

The more we advanced in the crisis, the more we had the impression of witnessing an unacceptable misunderstanding. I imagine that many Christians had lived through similar suffering: all those who, enthralled and deeply moved by Jesus's message of love, then saw their "brothers" persecute the Jews, burn heretics at the stake, preach in favor of the Crusades, or enslave entire defenseless populations, in the name of Christ.

We, whose hearts embraced when reading the admirable poems of Rumi, al-Hallaj[2] or Ibn Arabi[3] knew well that Islam, in its profound nature, could not belong to the fundamentalists. No more than the real Christianity could be that of the grand inquisitors of an earlier era or the fundamentalists of today. We knew well, to paraphrase Carlo Carretto,[4] that if theology divides, mys-

---

2. Al-Hallaj (858–922). Sufi mystic from Baghdad, executed by the authorities for heresy.

3. Ibn Arabi (1165–1240). Sufi mystic, philosopher, and scholar from Andalusian Spain, who traveled extensively in the Arab world and died in Damascus. Often referred to as the "Greatest Sheikh" for his philosophical writings, including developing the notion of unity of being, that all being is one (including the Divine) and everything is part of a single whole.

4. Carlo Carretto (1910–1988). Italian monk, author, and mystic who spent ten years as a hermit in Algeria during the war for independence from France. On his return to Italy, he moved to Spello, Umbria, where his order settled in a former Franciscan convent, welcoming people of all faiths, believers or not, who "wished

ticism unites the people of all traditions and, at a certain level of existence, all believers undergo the same experience.

For us, these interviews with Eva de Vitray-Meyerovitch were truly privileged moments. For us as Christians who feel comfortable in our tradition, it was a joy to encounter, through this exceptional woman, the Islam that we love: the Islam of the mystics, the Islam of tenderness.

Rachel and Jean-Pierre Cartier

---

to spend a period of reflection and search for faith lived in prayer, in manual work and in the exchange of experiences."

I had a very Catholic childhood. In May, during the month of the feast of the Virgin Mary, I went with my grandmother and took my first Communion. I believe I can say that I was a very pious little girl. I couldn't even imagine that life could be otherwise.

The Interviews

I

- **Without even thinking about it, the first question that came to us was the following: How could a young woman, born into the French aristocracy and educated by nuns, become a Muslim? What happened and why?**

I am not the only one to have made this journey. I have several friends, both men and women, who, brought up like me in the most traditional Catholicism, were attracted to Islam. My path is not as extraordinary as you seem to think.

I believe I was very influenced by one of my grandmothers, who was Scottish, of the Anglican Church. She converted to Catholicism to marry my grandfather. She often told me that in her eyes, going from high church Anglicanism to Catholicism consisted simply of accepting the Pope, which was not a big deal.

- **And she converted to marry?**

My grandfather wanted to be married in the Catholic Church. What always struck me about my grandmother was her basic honesty. She had this Puritanism that I have had occasion to admire in others, a bedrock notion of honesty, where being less than honest was considered cheating. To the point that to her, the innocent white lie was considered something very serious. I believe this influenced me a lot.

I had a very Catholic childhood. In May, during the month of the feast of the Virgin Mary, I went with my grandmother and took my first Communion. I believe I can say that I was a very pious little girl. I couldn't even imagine that life could be otherwise.

- **Were you educated by nuns?**

In part. By sisters in private schools after the 1905 law concerning congregations.[1] I must say I found the nuns rather annoying as a child.

• In Paris?

First in Boulogne, at a boarding school for proper young ladies. I then continued my studies in a private school located near Notre Dame at a school for young girls from well-to-do families where the atmosphere was very traditional.

• Did you suffer from it?

Not really. In fact, it didn't bother me too much because for me, faith went beyond this conformity, beyond this mold into which they wanted to pour us. [On Sundays] we went to Mass and, on leaving, we went to buy cakes at the pastry shop, simple things like that, but I was living something else. At eighteen, I imagined I wanted to be a Carmelite nun.[2] Today I think that I would have been a very bad Carmelite.

I continued my studies, did my high school diploma specializing in Latin and Greek, and then I studied law. Afterwards I began a doctorate in philosophy, but I'm jumping ahead . . .

• And during your studies, were you still a very Catholic little girl?

No, because the Catholicism I had been taught posed many problems for me.

• At which point, approximately?

From around 1925-30, I suffered from the atmosphere of conformity. Whenever I talked about my problems to the priests, they inevitably told me that it wasn't good to have doubts and that I should pray to the Lord to remove them from me. In fact, they

---

1. After the 1789 French Revolution, where the Church had sided with the monarchy, priests and members of religious orders all became civil servants, thus under the control of the government until 1905, when the law on the relationship between religions and the State was passed.

2. The Carmelite Order of nuns is a cloistered order focusing on contemplation, prayer, and community. Its name is derived from Mount Carmel in the Holy Land, said to be where Elijah lived. The Order, including friars as well as nuns, is considered inspired and guided by Elijah and the Virgin Mary. Two nuns from the Order, St. Teresa of Avila (1515-1582) from Spain and St. Thérèsa of Lisieux (1873-1897) from France, have been given the title Doctor of the Church, one of Catholicism's highest honors.

didn't give me anything satisfying as a response. Their authoritarianism made me even more uncomfortable. Given my desire not to cheat, it was impossible for me to set aside all the things that disturbed me. As a result, I had the impression of not being able to be truly faithful to my tradition.

When I was eighteen and had just started studying philosophy, this discomfort became intolerable. I had the feeling that to satisfy a need for religious experience, I had put into parentheses all that disturbed me. There was something impure in that, a little like a physical desire that is not accompanied by love.

- **Just what did you put into parentheses?**

All the dogma of the Catholic Church. I had studied enough history to read about the councils and to know, for example, that the earliest Gospels that we possess date from the 4th century and that even these were translations of translations. I had studied enough Greek to know that there could be a big difference between a Hellenistic expression and a Semitic expression.

- **Could you give us an example?**

Take for example, the very important phrase *Son of God*. In Greek, the term utilized really means the actual son or infant. In Isaiah, on the other hand, it signified the "Servant (of God)." Those meanings are not at all the same thing. There was there something very vague that had been hardened by subsequent declarations from church councils that I had a hard time accepting.

To stay within my "community," I would have had to disregard facts, and as I already said, I just couldn't keep putting things like this into parentheses. Not long ago I met a young priest, very nice, who made this strange declaration to me: "I feel profoundly Christian, but when I say mass, I don't believe in transubstantiation." If I were a priest, I'd rather throw myself out the window than say Mass without believing in transubstantiation.

- **Could we say you were especially uncomfortable with dogma?**

You could say that. I had a hard time putting up with the authoritarianism of the Roman Catholic Church. I found myself asking myself questions like, "By what right did the Church proclaim the dogma about the assumption of Mary in 1943?"[3]

In my eyes, the Church has the right to make value judgments, but not absolute judgments of fact. To give you an example, when was the Church wrong: when it condemned Galileo or when it rehabilitated him? All this disturbed me horribly and I said to myself more and more often, "If I stay just because I want to go to Communion on Sunday morning, it's cheating. It's perfectly impure."

- **But at the same time, when you went to Communion, did you experience something profound?**

It's hard for me to remember what my feelings were at the time, but I'm afraid it was a little sentimental. I was perfectly sincere, but without fully realizing it, I mainly felt the need for a religious experience.

- **You were a young girl who asked herself many questions.**

I never stopped asking questions!

- **Did you have a spiritual guide?**

Not particularly. I went to Confession just about any place, but every time I was a little saddened by these continuous mental restrictions of things I couldn't say. Even today, I recently had occasion to have a conversation with an important theologian. You may say that fifty years have passed since my doubts as a young girl and that Vatican II has taken place, but still, I was completely stupefied to hear this priest say to me, in response to one of my questions, "But who still really believes in Purgatory, in Hell, or in original sin? In my eyes, they are the inventions of theologians to explain weaknesses in human nature."

Really, faced with this brilliant man who is not at all criticized by his church, I couldn't help but ask, "Well, what's left if he removes all that? He simply did away with all that's disturbing." I couldn't just do away with what disturbed me.

---

3. From as early as the 5th century, groups of Christians celebrated a holiday for the assumption of Mary (that is, her not dying, but being taken up into heaven). The church dogma making this belief official doctrine was proclaimed in 1950 by Pope Pius XII, not 1943 as stated above.

- **You perceived that as a form of intellectual dishonesty?**

Perhaps I did, because personally I would certainly have had the impression of pretending. Going to Communion under these circumstances would seem sacrilegious to me. That's why I preferred to drop it all. I made a radical break.

- **All the same, this need for a religious experience always remained deep inside you.**

No doubt for that reason I appeased my hunger a bit by reading the mystics. I also took some Sanskrit and studied a lot of Indian philosophy, but that didn't satisfy me either. I nonetheless felt a little more freedom because at least there was no clergy, no hierarchy to tell me, "No salvation outside the church."

I persisted. I submerged myself, for example, in the Bhagavad Gita, which has remained one of my bedside books. I also studied Buddhism, but all this was a little beyond me, a bit bookish. I had a lot of admiration for Buddhism, for its universal compassion, for its love of animals, for its absence of dogma, but it all remained a little distant. In addition, even if I knew a little Sanskrit, I didn't know any Pali or Tibetan. To do things seriously, I would have had to go to Tibet to study with a spiritual guide, and that was quite impossible for me at the time.

- **Perhaps that was not your calling?**

In any case, it wasn't my destiny. I have a friend who is a Buddhist and she is a truly exceptional woman, but she lived in Nepal, has been to Tibet, and had prominent Tibetan teachers. That kind of journey was even more difficult for me to consider because I got married when I was only twenty-two, well before World War II.

My husband was my age and we were both students, both passionate about our studies. He was finishing his engineering degree and I my doctorate, with symbolism in Plato as a dissertation topic. I also took courses in psychiatry for three years to try to establish a distinction between normal symbolic thought and pathological symbolic thought. It was a beautiful subject that I eventually abandoned to deal with Muslim philosophy.

- We will get back to that in a moment. What struck us about you is that you have spent your entire life as a devoted student. You seem to have been born to study.

I love it. I believe the most beautiful gift a good fairy can bestow on a child is to give her or him curiosity. Everything interests me and I, who am already quite old, believe that old age consists of saying, "I will never learn Chinese or nuclear physics." Even learning manual skills fascinates me. I would like to learn pottery or cabinet making.

- You don't seriously want to learn nuclear physics now, do you?

Certainly not, if only because I was always unable to solve equations! I often say that old age, in my eyes, starts when you lose curiosity. I am still passionately curious.

Indeed, even though I'm not a physicist, I have met prominent nuclear physicists. Before the war, I worked as a young administrator in the laboratory of Frédéric Joliot-Curie who, with his wife Irène, obtained the Nobel Prize in 1935 for their discovery of artificial radioactivity. I was living in an extraordinary period then.

- But you were not a scientist, were you?

Not at all. In fact, Joliot-Curie always teased me, saying, "Oh, you poor literary types! I can read Shakespeare as well as you, but you can't understand differential calculus." I bowed my head and said, "That's very true, sir."

We were very good friends. His wife and he were adorable. They were at the Collège de France,[4] right near where I now live, in this apartment which has always been my home in Paris, and where all of my books are. At that time, Frédéric Joliot-Curie was in the process of working on the atomic bomb. I remember he never stopped asking the Minister of War for a site in the Sahara to undertake the first tests. But the minister always refused.

On May 11, 1940, he called me and said, "I can't say anything.

---

4. Prestigious institution founded in 1530 by Francis I, and later supported by Louis XIV, where initially fifty French scholars and selected foreign scholars were chosen to lecture and do research, usually for a year.

The Germans are at the edge of Paris. Take your son, your money, your jewelry if you have any, and come quickly. There's a car that will take you far from Paris." In that car there was the one and only bottle of heavy water that existed at the time. I later learned their orders were to commit suicide rather than to reveal what it was. As for me, they could have questioned me because I didn't know anything.

The car dropped me in Loiret, at the home of one of my childhood friends, who later became the mother-in-law of my older son.

This reminds me that a while ago, the superior of a Benedictine abbey came to see me. He had written me a friendly letter in a powerful handwriting, telling me he was writing a book on Muslim mysticism and that he wanted to meet with me . . . At the end, I said to him, "Father, don't you think it's a shame that history has missed so many opportunities for rendezvous? There were the Templars, the Elizabethans, and the precursors of Shakespeare with all this universalism that was later hidden." He smiled warmly and said to me, "The only consolation, madam, is to think that we are all saying the same thing."

II

- So here you are, plunged in the war, escaping from Paris with a baby on your hands. Was your husband at the front?

He was in the middle of his military service when war was declared. After the (French) defeat, he joined the Free French Forces and I went four years without any news from him. Joliot-Curie was in America and I no longer had work in Paris. So I lived alone with my baby in the Corrèze, near Brive. I stayed there throughout the war. I saw the German division that massacred the people in Oradour march by in front of me.[1]

Soon after I first arrived, I was visited by the Gestapo in the middle of the night. They were looking for my husband, who had lived briefly in Brive just after the truce between the Germans and occupied France. At that time he had a food ration card which allowed the Germans to track his location, but he left France for Spain and then London. People ask me if I believe in miracles. Indeed I do, because that night when the Gestapo arrived at my door, I lived through one! It was three in the morning. The brave people I lived with had gone away to a wedding. I was alone in the house with my little three-year old son.

When I opened the door, I found myself opposite someone who resembled Frankenstein. He didn't even look mean, it was worse. He was wearing the SS uniform with its skull and crossbones and he looked perfectly clean and proper, but with eyes as vacant as if he were drugged. I had the impression that if someone had said to him, "Go cut up your mother into small pieces," he would have gone right off to do it, after shouting, "Heil Hitler!" His companion was a simple soldier of the Wehrmacht who looked very uncomfortable with himself. They asked me where my husband was. At that moment it was like seeing myself in a movie. There was part of me that was dying of fright. I said to

---

1. Over six hundred civilians were killed in the village of Oradour on June 10, 1944.

myself, "If they take me and torture me, I might be capable of denouncing comrades in the Resistance. You never know what you might do or say under torture. If they deport me, the baby will die and my husband will find no one when the war is over." I was terrified, but at the same time, another part of me heard me speaking in a sort of Berlin slang that I didn't know at all. I remember having pronounced this phrase, "My husband probably ran off with some broad, but I couldn't care less."

- **Did you know German?**

A little, but the German of Kant and Hegel, not at all the language of the slums of Berlin. In this strange vision of myself, I was stupefied to hear myself talking and at the same time feeling something in my heart that asked forgiveness from my husband for accusing him that way. I saw then, on the phlegmatic face of the German officer, a little glimmer of something human and he said that I spoke German very well. "Obviously!" I muttered indignantly to myself, after which he elbowed his buddy and said, "She's kidding around, she has nothing to hide." They left and I found myself panting. I was seized with such a case of the shakes that I tore up a pack of cigarettes that were otherwise very precious because I was exchanging them for bread. I never understood what happened to me in that moment. That's why I believe in miracles.

- **And since then, you have never spoken Berlin slang?**

Never. Indeed, even today I don't know how to say the German word for a "broad."

- **There were many members of the Resistance in the Corrèze. Hadn't you been contacted by the Resistance?**

Yes, of course. We had hidden people, but I don't like to sound boastful. I was able to see from close hand the horrors of war. As I told you, I watched Das Reich march by, the division responsible for hanging people in Tulle and the massacre in Oradour. The house where I lived was near the Kommandantur (Command Headquarters), where people cried out as they were tortured.

Even then, I was able to save a German officer because he really deserved it. I didn't have much money at the time. I was part of the Ministry of Education, but there was no branch of the ministry in Brive. I was lucky to be able to get a job at Philips as a documentation specialist and, given that I didn't have an enormous salary, I placed an ad in a newspaper to give lessons in Latin, Greek, English, or French. Right away, a German officer contacted me to improve his French. I wanted to refuse, but he looked like he wouldn't take it very well. "Your ad only came out this morning," he said. I was all the more embarrassed because the people I lived with didn't want to hear about receiving a German officer in their home. He cut through my hesitation by saying, "You'll need to come to my hotel. You see, I need to stay near my telephone because I work in communications."

I can still see myself arriving at this hotel. I was very young and timid. At the reception, when I pronounced the name of the German officer, the French lady who ran the hotel and was likely its owner looked at me as if I were nothing. I explained what was happening, saying I was scared to death and added, "If I call, come quickly."

In the end, everything worked out well. The officer was very kind, very courteous. He had a brother who had just been killed on the Russian front. We didn't exactly have friendly relations, but he was always very proper. He was of Yugoslav origin.

At the time of the liberation, I saw that they were putting him into a truck and I testified in his favor. That's how I saved him. I thought it was the right thing to do.

• So you were well connected within the Resistance?

A little, well enough in any case to receive one of the first transportation coupons to take me to Paris. I had received, in fact, a card from my husband saying he had just arrived. That's how we found each other after four years of separation. He had been wounded during the French campaign. We lost absolutely everything, our apartment was empty, and we had to start over from scratch. Very quickly we had a second child. I experienced a tough period because during the war I had exhausted myself by walking ten kilometers a day to go to work. I had a severe case of anemia and was sick for four years.

Of course, that was not enough to stifle my thirst for learning. I managed to pass the entrance exam for what was about the equivalent today of the National School for Administration, which allowed me to serve in one of the elite branches of the civil service as a manager. I chose the National Center for Scientific Research

(CNRS), where, while continuing to prepare my dissertation on symbolism in the works of Plato, I directed the social sciences service. Later, in order to have more time for my dissertation, I asked to be transferred to a research position.

- **Social sciences, to the lay person, sounds awfully vague. Can you tell us exactly what you were doing at the CNRS?**

I organized conferences, I met people and reviewed their applications to direct them toward the right committee. All my life, I've been fortunate to meet fascinating people.

I already told you about Joliot-Curie. I found him after the war when he was named Chairman of the Atomic Energy Commission [in France]. That's when they decided to replace him at CNRS with two directors, one for physical sciences and the other for social sciences. I was the assistant to the social sciences director and, when he died in 1954, I replaced him at the head of this service. I took over this direction in a bizarre fashion because it was a position that, administratively, I didn't have a right to. I moved into the office of the director and took over the function. It was very time consuming, to such an extent that I didn't have any time for my dissertation. When I realized the situation, I asked to be transferred to a research position.

- **Being a woman never caused you any problems in these circles?**

Not at all. It was much less difficult among civil servants than in the private sector. First of all, we had the same salary as the men. It is true that at that time there were not many women who did what I did. When I obtained my law degree, I was first in my class. Obviously that helped me a little with respect to the young men, but I always worked very hard.

- **Did you stay at the CNRS long?**

Till the end of my career. But I didn't always stay in my office. I was often sent on assignments, including being seconded temporarily to other government organizations.[2]

---

2. Ranking Civil Service employees in most countries may be assigned to other branches of government to develop their knowledge as well as share their specialized skills.

• **Could you give us an example?**

In 1969, because I knew the Arab world well, I was given a five-year appointment as a professor at al-Azhar University in Cairo where I taught comparative philosophy. I took a theme, the notion of time for example, and I examined how it had been treated by Western philosophy and by Oriental philosophy.

Egypt at that time was a paradise. You can't imagine what Cairo was like then. I lived with Egyptian friends, translated Rumi, and out of my window I saw the Nile and boats that had the same sails they had at the time of the pharaohs. Since then they have built all those infamous high-rise residential buildings.

It was the good, sweet life. We could stroll around. And there was Egyptian hospitality. It still exists, but now the Egyptians have too many economic problems, population pressures, and intolerable traffic jams. Life has become too difficult. Some of my students and I have still stayed in touch as friends.

I returned to France in 1973 and from then on, I had an enormous number of missions abroad, to Libya, to Kuwait, to Saudi Arabia, and again to Egypt.

• **What did these missions consist of?**

Most of the time, I was responsible for organizing conferences and lectures[3] in these countries.

• **On what subjects?**

The subjects varied. In Kuwait, they asked me to give lectures on Islam; in Libya, on Sufism. Or a comparison between Western and Oriental philosophy. I went to Iran during the time of the Shah, to Sudan, to Morocco, and to Turkey many times.

Indeed, I have always had a predilection for Turkey. I've been to Konya at least ten times. But I have also worked in Morocco ten times and fifteen times in Algeria. At the same time, I was writing or translating books. I believe I've traveled abroad at least forty times.

---

3. In English, *conference* usually implies multiple speakers, while in French it may mean a presentation or lecture by a recognized expert, called a *conférencier/conférencière*, speaking on a subject in their field, usually followed by questions and answers. In English, a press conference is an example of a conference with a single speaker providing information and responding to questions.

- **Tell us about your books. What was the first one?**

Translations from English that were, I must admit, rather elementary. After the war, my husband was a student again and, as I said, we had nothing. We didn't even have a bank account. I tried not to do just anything, only those things that interested me, books on sociology, and a book on China that was produced by the Swiss publishing firm Payot. I worked during the day, and at night I did translations.

I also personally wrote a book on Henry VIII at the request of the publishing firm Julliard which they asked me to do because they knew I was an English language specialist and interested in English history. This book was part of a collection edited by Georges Pernoud[4] and was called *There's Always a Reporter*. It was translated into German and Finnish.

- **Were you particularly interested in Henry VIII?**

No, it was Georges Pernoud who proposed the topic. He was looking for an English language specialist. You know the English of the time of Henry VIII is a bit like the French of the time of Charles V. I can read it because I also wrote a book about Christine de Pizan,[5] which allowed me to make the comparison. I was brought up on English literature. With my grandmother, about whom I've spoken so often, I learned English before French.

- **But Henry VIII was not really a nice person . . .**

Absolutely not, he was Bluebeard.[6] An evil man, but the era was fascinating. There was Thomas More.[7] Then, under Elizabeth, there

---

4. Georges Pernoud (1947 to present). French journalist, editor, producer and host of an ongoing weekly series about the sea, *Thalassa*.

5. Christine de Pizan, also spelled Pisan (1364–1430). She later moved with her parents to the French court of Charles VI. Married at the age of 15, her husband died 10 years later, and she began writing to provide for her two children and her mother. One of the world's first women professional writers, she used her pen to criticize stereotypes about women and is considered an early feminist.

6. Bluebeard was a fictional wife-murderer in *Tales of Mother Goose* (*Les Contes de ma mère l'Oye*) written, collected and published in 1697 by the French author Charles Perraut (1628-1703).

7. Thomas More (1478–1535). English humanist scholar, lawyer, and statesman, executed by Henry VIII.

was a tradition of hermeticism[8] and the alchemists.[9] And also that extraordinary person who was the Cardinal de Kues.[10] This German cardinal back in 1437 recommended holding a council among Jews, Christians, and Muslims. He read the Qur'an in Arabic and wrote absolutely astounding things, for example:

"When the Qur'an says that you shouldn't say 'Son of God,' it is quite right because that leads to confusion. When the Qur'an says, 'When you speak of God, don't talk about the Trinity,' it is quite right because people will believe there are three gods."

There are thousands of unfortunates who were burned alive for saying less than this.

There was also Marsile Ficin,[11] Arnaud de Villeneuve,[12] and certain alchemists who were very close to the principles of Islam. This movement was completely stifled during the 15th century by the horrible Borgia pope.

Nevertheless, over the centuries this current of hermetic thought continued to run underground, reemerged at the end of the Enlightenment, and blossomed during German Romanticism.

This reminds me that a while ago, the superior of a Benedictine abbey came to see me. He had written me a friendly letter in a powerful handwriting, telling me he was writing a book on Muslim mysticism and that he wanted to meet with me. I was all the more flattered because he was coming to Paris just to see me. When he arrived, he was initially rather cold but very bright and informed, and we quickly wound up talking like brother and sister. At the end, I said to him, "Father, don't you think it's a shame that

---

8. A set of philosophical, religious, and mystical beliefs based on the writings of Hermes Trismegistus (historic and/or mythical person) from Egypt. He is mentioned in Plutarch's writings in the 1st century C.E

9. Philosophical, physical, and metaphysical study of nature, sometimes erroneously limited to the attempt to turn ordinary metals into gold. Alchemy existed in many parts of the ancient world (Egypt, Greece, Rome, Mesopotamia, Persia), including in the writings of Hermes Trismegistus, but was also documented in India, Japan, and China. Its practice was also prevalent in Medieval Europe, Elizabethan England, and the Islamic world.

10. Cardinal Nicholas Cusa or Nicholas of Kues (1401-1464). 15th century German mystic, philosopher, astronomer, theologian, and jurist.

11. Marsile Ficin (1422–1499). Italian philosopher who translated Plato as well as key works on hermeticism.

12. Arnaud de Villeneuve (1238–1311 or 1313). French physician, chemist, and scholar who knew Latin, Hebrew, and Arabic.

history has missed so many opportunities for rendezvous? There were the Templars, the Elizabethans, and the precursors of Shakespeare with all this universalism that was later hidden." He smiled warmly and said to me, "The only consolation, madam, is to think that we are all saying the same thing."

- **All Benedictines wouldn't say the same thing. We know some who are extremely obscurantist.**[13]

That depends on the abbot. Personally, I have lots of Benedictine friends. They are generally very open.

- **We have talked a little about your personal life, and while doing this, we have jumped ahead. I'd like us to go back a little and for you to tell us about your encounter with Islam.**

---

13. In 1509, the Holy Roman Emperor Maximillian (1486-1519) gave permission to burn all copies of the Talmud (Jewish law and ethics) known to be in the Holy Roman Empire (926–1806 C.E.). *Letters of Obscure Men (Epistolæ Obscurorum Virorum)* satirized the Dominican arguments for burning "un-Christian" works. In the 18th century, Enlightenment philosophers applied the term *obscurantist* to any enemy of intellectual enlightenment and the liberal diffusion of knowledge.

III

To speak clearly about my encounter with Islam, I need to go back to immediately after the war. I had seen many atrocious things during the war and that caused me to ask myself many questions without finding answers. For reasons that I explained to you, returning to my Catholic origins would have felt like avoiding the real issues.

I was thirsty for absolute principles, and I was not feeling good about myself. I can't say that I was praying because I didn't yet believe in much. It was more like an SOS that a boat sends out in the night, wondering if someone will hear it.

My inner request was heard when I was in my office at CNRS when one of my good friends arrived whom I hadn't seen for fifteen years. He was a well-known Muslim with whom I had studied Sanskrit. As an aside, I have extraordinary memories of that period during which I was privileged to dine next to Gandhi and to meet lots of fascinating people. Among them was this friend, who was an Indian classmate in France, a marvelous former student of Einstein.

After his return to India, we continued to correspond from time to time. I learned that he had become rector of the University of Islamabad and that he had four children. And now suddenly, after all these years, he arrived in my office. He had had a lot of trouble finding me.

We talked a long time. He had to equip his laboratories and due to his positive memories of France, he wanted to give it preference for his orders. When he left me, he gave me a little book, saying, "I know that you have always been interested in religious questions. Read this book. It's the best work of our greatest spiritual guide, Iqbal." I replied, "Thank you very much, dear friend." And I left the book on my table where it was quickly covered by papers. I was really very busy then.

A little later, I finally opened this famous book. I saw that it was entitled, *Reconstruction of Religious Thought in Islam* and that it was in

English. I wanted to just skim it, but from the first pages I couldn't put it down. I suddenly had the impression that it answered all my questions. I found the universalism so long desired, this idea that fundamentally all revelation must be one, that two and two are indeed four everywhere and that these numbers always represent the same truth, whether they are in Aztec, Chinese, or Arabic numerals. Yes, one truth. The Qur'an says nothing but this.

I loved this book so much that I immediately began to translate it. I loved Iqbal and a certain Rumi that he talked about all the time.

- **You say that so simply, but it's truly extraordinary. It sounds like the simple fact of reading this book by Iqbal with one stroke completely changed your life. We'd like to know a little more about him and his book.**

You know, for a book to change your life you have to be ready for it. I was already on the path of open questioning, of personal interpretation, of individual research. I found all that embodied in this great thinker. And then I was happy to see that I was not alone, lost on a side street, but that I was situated, without knowing it, within an established tradition. And all this without having to give up anything! I didn't deny the Torah and the New Testament. I simply left behind those things that always irritated me: the decisions of church councils, dogmas from men meeting in Rome to decide that God was like this or like that.

Up till that moment, I had been uncomfortable. I would ask myself why I gave myself the right to criticize things established for so long. When I understood that a quarter of humanity thought like me, I suddenly felt less strange. In fact, I found a clear response to all the questions I had been asking myself. Or if you prefer, this book gave me a nudge. I had no idea that this could be Islam. I once heard [the French philosopher] Roger Garaudy say that you could do a doctorate in philosophy without ever having heard of the Arab thinkers. That's absolutely correct, and that's scandalous. At that time, we read Kant, Hegel, and a lot of other philosophers, but specifically not Muslim philosophers. That's why my discovery of Islam through a book by Iqbal was such an event for me. I suddenly had nothing to hide, nothing to avoid talking about. There was no one to say to me, "If you don't believe this way, you're out of line." What a relief!

III

- **Tell us more about Iqbal.**

I could talk to you about him for hours. He is one of the spiritual founders of Pakistan, a great philosopher, a very great thinker, a lawyer, and a poet who wrote equally well in Persian, English, and Urdu. He is considered one of the greatest reformers of Islam. He wrote his dissertation in Munich on metaphysics in Persia. I translated this dissertation, as well as almost all his work in English and Persian. I also just finished an anthology of a certain number of his important texts at the request of the ambassador of Pakistan.

- **Did he know the West well?**

He lived and studied here a long time. He was a great friend of Bergson[1] and of Massignon,[2] who was my teacher. He was at Cambridge and was part of the roundtable that founded Pakistan. His book, *Reconstruction of Religious Thought in Islam*, presents a totally modern view of Islam, while well within the Islamic tradition.

- **Did you know him?**

No, because he died in 1938, but I know his son very well. In 1950, he gave me permission to translate the works of his father. I see him often in conferences and seminars. He is a remarkable man who is now president of the Court of Appeals of his country. It's a great pleasure for me to be able to speak with people of this stature because they possess a double culture: Western culture as well as their profound religious conviction. There is no contradiction.

What struck me with Iqbal's vision of the world is his constant search for unity, a constant desire to reconcile the fundamental principles of the Qur'an and the discoveries of science. His friend Bergson said that we needed to bring a little more soul to Western culture. That's exactly what he wanted to do.

He was troubled by the disarray of humanity in the 20th century and felt lost in the middle of the universe, haunted by that metaphysical anguish that Teilhard de Chardin talks about.

---

1. Henri Bergson (1859–1941). French scholar, philosopher, and author who taught at the Collège de France.
2. Louis Massignon (1883–1962). French scholar of Islam and Christian ecumenist who taught at the Collège de France.

- **So is he a pessimistic thinker?**

Not at all, because he believes in humanity and, to a certain extent, in progress, which can be good on the condition that human beings manage to get beyond the geocentricity and medieval anthropomorphism that imprison them still. "No form of reality," he proclaimed, "is as powerful, as vivifying and as magnificent as the human spirit." He sees people becoming, in the process of evolution, the complete, fully realized human being the Sufis talk about [*insan al-kamil*], that is to say the accomplished person who knows how to use the wholeness that she or he has acquired to help other individuals move forward.

- **In terms of evolution, that no doubt means that time is a very important notion for him.**

Of course. He says it himself, the problem of time, like indeed the problem of space, is a question of life and death. "Time," he writes in one of his last letters, "is a great benediction. If on the one hand it brings death and destruction, on the other hand it is the source of creation and fertility. It is time that reveals the possibilities hidden in everything. The possibility of changing present conditions is the greatest value and the greatest treasure of humanity."

- **In this perspective, there can be no racism or nationalism.**

Exactly right. I love to cite this phrase of his, "There are no Afghans, Turks, or sons of Tartars. We are all the fruits of the same garden, from the same trunk, we are the blossoming of the same springtime."

It's this openness, this tolerance inherent in the depths of his abandon to the Divine that makes him an authentic Sufi.

- **You speak about him as you have spoken about your beloved Rumi.**

Because I see between them a startling resemblance. I once said that Rumi served as his initiator and guide just as Virgil enabled Dante to realize his celestial voyage. They are both poets, both philosophers, both mystics. Both had the same vision of evolution, whose supreme fruit should be the completely realized human being. Both were fascinated by science, and both swear that love is the only force that moves the universe. Only love is eternal.

All his life, this thinker was an eternal student and a man of action. He wrote a doctoral thesis in Munich, taught philosophy and English literature in India, and taught Arabic literature in England. All these contacts with the two worlds made him a mediator and quickly gave him the stature of a statesman. Because he was also a lawyer, he was elected president of the Indian Union Muslim League, created in 1906, and a member of the roundtable conference held in London in 1931 to elaborate a constitution for India. Later his work played an important role in the creation of Pakistan.[3]

He died in Lahore on May 21, 1938. Just before he died, with a smile on his lips, after pronouncing the name of God, he recited these verses:

> The melody in flight can come back or not
> The breeze can blow again from the Hijaz or not
> The days of the humble dervish come to their end
> Another visionary will return or not.

- **You once told us that there was a parallel between the thinking of Iqbal and that of Teilhard de Chardin. Can you say a little more about this idea?**

Iqbal knew Father Teilhard personally. They couldn't fail to get along because the great theme of Iqbal is that everything that rises converges. That should remind you of something. If everything converges, that means that if you go to the end of your Buddhism, your Christianity, or your Islam, you can only find yourself in submission to Divine Spirit.

- **And you also knew Teilhard de Chardin personally?**

Yes, and I had the privilege of making the first radio broadcast about him and of writing the first articles about him. The Roman Catholic Church publicly humiliated him and forbade him to speak

---

3. Later, Iqbal felt that the Muslims would be better served by a separate state, Pakistan (then consisting of two Muslim regions, on the eastern and western sides of India). He also influenced Jinnah, afterwards to become Pakistan's first president, to support separation from India. In a letter to Jinnah, he wrote, "A separate federation of Muslim Provinces, reformed on the lines I have suggested . . . is the only course by which we can secure a peaceful India and save Muslims from the domination of Non-Muslims."

at the Collège de France.

I wrote the first article for an Italian review and, before sending it off, I scrupulously went to see Father d'Oince, who had been his spiritual director. I remember saying to him, "You understand I am not Catholic and certainly not a theologian. I don't want to make comments that could be used against Father Teilhard, for whom I have great esteem." He read my article and I will never forget the subsequent conversation I had with him.

You have to understand that I was brought up as a good little girl in appearance, but I was not at all conventional. I was twelve years old when I managed to ask my confessor if it was bad to believe in reincarnation. You can imagine his response. I always asked the questions you shouldn't ask. So I asked Father d'Oince:

"How can you explain that Father Teilhard never talks about Hell?"

"Do you believe in it?" he asked.

"No, but I'm not an authority. Maybe we could make up for it with the idea of Purgatory."[4]

I will always remember his reaction. He looked at me with a gentle and slightly ironic smile and said to me, "Madam, you sound just like a nun." It was adorable.

- **While we're on this subject, what does Islam say about Hell?**

There is no eternal Hell. It's even inconceivable. At the most there's a purification, if you will, corresponding to Purgatory.

- **Another word about Teilhard de Chardin. For us he was a very great person.**

For me, too. In all the prefaces that I wrote, I cited with love Teilhard de Chardin and this essential expression according to which all that rises converges.

- **Would you say he was a good Muslim?**

A very good Muslim. No one has ever surrendered to the will of God more than he.

---

4. Purgatory (Latin: *purgatorium* via Anglo-Norman and Old French) is an intermediate state after physical death for expiatory purification. Roman Catholic doctrine holds that this state exists and that those being purified can be helped by the prayers of the living.

- **So your discovery of Iqbal was essential.**

Exactly.

- **Can we say that it was this encounter that led you to convert to Islam?**

Certainly, to the extent that I was already ready. But after all, don't think that it was so simple. I asked myself a lot of questions. I said to myself that it was all well and good to be enthralled by Islam, but you can't change your tradition the way you change a shirt. It could have been that after all, my knowledge of Christianity was very worldly, very aristocratic, and very typical of a young lady from a good family. I said to myself that Christians were not idiots and that perhaps I had understood things wrong. So, out of concern for honesty, I decided to take three years to study the Bible before deciding anything.

- **Where did you go?**

To the Sorbonne. I had taken courses on scriptural interpretation with Oscar Culmann, and I also had to take a few courses in theology because you can't interpret scripture without having at least some notions of theology. But I didn't take a formal course in theology. Oscar Culmann was a Protestant, a professor at the Sorbonne and at the University of Basel, with a good feeling for Catholicism. Just as there are Catholics with a Protestant sensitivity, there are Protestants with a Catholic sensitivity. He was perfectly honest and knew Greek very well. We worked on the Gospels, reading them word by word, and I did this for three years.

- **This does not seem to have convinced you of the superiority of Christianity.**

My studies were not at all about that. They were fascinating, but perhaps a little too intellectual an approach. It was not really what I expected.

Of course, I learned a lot of things, but endless objections came up from within me.

- **Like what, for example?**

For example, there were church councils that never stopped irritating me because they reached decisions in an authoritarian manner. Everything to do with the Virgin Mary, for example, or at least the expression *Mother of God*. What does it mean? We have to be clear about this. It could mean the mother of Christ, the mother of Jesus, all right. But Mother of God, that certainly causes a problem. Mother of the Absolute? Would that mean that St. Anne [the mother of the Virgin Mary] was the grandmother of the Absolute? This interpretation seemed very simplistic to me and demonstrated that sort of hiatus that exists between the evangelic message and what was drawn from it. It often occurred to me to say, during these three years of study, "Really, when you think of billions of light years and galaxies, it's certainly like looking at things from the wrong end of the telescope!"

I quickly had the feeling that Islam denied nothing of what was essential. The Qur'an recognizes the virgin birth of Jesus and has great respect for the Virgin Mary. The annunciation made to Mary in the Qur'an is the same as in the book of Luke. All this is clear, but when, twenty centuries later, the Church decides to proclaim the dogma of the Assumption and to require the faithful to believe it, that was a sore point for me.

It was interesting for me to see that there was a precursor to the book of Matthew, and that the book of Matthew itself is filled with Aramaicisms.

- **But it was written in Aramaic.**

Yes, but the Greek translation is filled with Aramaicisms. It's a little bit like someone who doesn't know English well who translates "What is the matter?" by "What is the substance?"

And then I was troubled by the way the Gospels are dated, by the fact that the oldest manuscript or the oldest part of a manuscript that we possess, located in the British Museum, is dated by carbon-14 testing as the beginning of the 2nd century. That text is only a very little fragment. The rest is much later.

In the end, studying the Bible raised more problems for me than it resolved.

- **Give us an example.**

I could give you many. Just to look at one, take the expression *Son of God*. In Greek we say *"Uios Theou."* What does that mean exactly? In Hebrew as in Arabic, there are two words for the word *son*, the physical son and the spiritual son. When you say to a little child,

"Son, go get me a pack of cigarettes," that doesn't mean he's your own son. In Greek, there's only one word for *son*. A choice had to be made, but who tells us it's the right choice? This is the type of problem that of course interested me, but I didn't attach too much importance to it.

I must admit that St. John of the Cross or Rumi meant more to me.

- **But you certainly made a significant effort.**

A worthy effort!

- **You took three years of your life for a principle. I find that to be remarkably honest.**

I told you that I had a grandmother who was a Puritan and she taught me not to cheat. For me it was impossible to put anything problematic aside, though many Catholics I know do just that to avoid conflicts.

- **I'd like to go into more detail. During these three years, you were, if you will, between Islam and Christianity, an ideal situation to draw a parallel between the two religions. Are they as irreconcilable, as antagonistic as we have been taught?**

That's a delicate question that forces us to talk a little about the problem of languages. Let's say at the beginning that what really struck me was that Islam doesn't rule out anything, doesn't deny anything, and accepts all revelation incarnated in an authentic book such as the Torah and the Gospels.

This question of languages is very important. We always talk about the "Religions of the Book" and the religion of the book par excellence is Islam, because it is based completely on a book. Tradition has only a secondary place. And because there is no church in Islam, no clergy, no authority responsible for determining "the Truth," everything goes back to the book. Tradition has a much bigger place in Judaism, while Christianity is based on the message of the Gospels, on the testimony of the first communities and, later, on the teachings of the church.

It is certainly not by chance that the three great languages of revelation in the world, Hebrew, Arabic, and Sanskrit, can be understood on several levels. My Jewish friends were telling me one day that Hebrew and Arabic are like those Russian dolls. The different meanings in them are nested inside each other. The meanings certainly can't be contradictory, but each person can read them according to their own intuition and their own intelligence.

- **According to their degree of evolution?**

Yes.

- **I don't understand very well. I need some examples.**

I could give you hundreds of examples. Take for example the famous *houris*, the miraculous [perpetually virgin] women that are waiting for believers in Paradise. We can see them in an absolutely anthropological fashion, like in the painting of the three Greek Muses of Proudhon.[5] But in fact, it's a word that also means "grace."

In the Qur'an, the word that means "water" also means "H_2O," "life," and "grace." Clearly for a Bedouin dying of thirst in the desert, water is H_2O, and life, as well as the grace that God sends.

- **So words can be read with several meanings. But isn't the same thing also true of the New Testament?**

The difference is that in the New Testament, the parables are at several levels. It's not the word itself and the word alone as in the Torah and the Qur'an. That comes, in my opinion, from the fact that the New Testament is an inspired book but not a revealed book in the same sense as the Torah or the Qur'an, where each letter is revealed.

Would you like another example of the importance attached to a word? You know, all the *surahs* [chapters] of the Qur'an begin with, "In the name of God, the Merciful and the Compassionate." In reality, it's a bad translation, but there isn't another one. The word *al-Rahman* comes from a Semitic root that means "womb." So Chouraqui,[6] who just finished a translation of the Qur'an which is a bit of a mishmash but has the immense advantage of going back to its origins, translates it as "uterine love." It's correct, no doubt,

---

5. Pierre-Paul Proudhon (1758–1823). French Romantic painter of *Apollo and the Nine Muses on Mount Parnassus*. Trained in the Classical style in France and Italy, he is also known for his allegorical and religious paintings, as well as portraits of the wealthy and the French court, including the wives of Napoleon.

6. André Chouraqui (1917–2007). Algerian-born French scholar, later Israeli, who translated the Hebrew Bible, the New Testament, and the Qur'an from their original languages (into French) with commentary.

but not very pretty. In reality, it means that God has the same tenderness for all creatures as a mother holding a child to her breast.

All the *surahs* in the Qur'an begin with these words except the ninth one, which is about repentance. Many commentators have asked why. Simply because in the idea of penitence, there is a notion of proximity. So if you repent – not just lip service, but in a state of true contrition – you are very, very near to God. So close that there is no need to say, "In the name of God, the Merciful and the Compassionate."

It's the only *surah* that doesn't start with this formula. You see, from this example, in Arabic as in Hebrew, each letter is important, each word has combined and multiple meanings, that each individual can read according to his or her own intelligence and attitude.

- **In these conditions, it isn't easy to read the Qur'an. Everyone can interpret it in their own way.**

The rule, if we can say rule, is to read it as if it had just at that moment been revealed to you personally. I say just at that moment because sometimes, on a second reading, you can read something else entirely. It's a process of savoring again and again that reminds me of the phrase used by several of my Muslim friends, "The Qur'an is our communion."

- **Can we say that Muslims compare Muhammad to Jesus?**

It would be more correct to say that they compare Muhammad to the Virgin Mary. Because the Prophet was not an educated man, he was illiterate. He had to be virgin with respect to any preconceived notions of cultures so the revelation could be inscribed on him as onto a blank slate: his personal knowledge would not act as a screen. In contrast, we compare the Qur'an to the human person of Jesus, who was himself the spokesperson or bearer of the Word.

- **One day you spoke to us about the symbol of a wheel. Isn't this the very symbol of the tolerance of true Islam?**

If you will, but to understand, you have to begin with the essential idea of acceptance. Whereas other religions bear the name of their founder or the country where they were born, Islam is the only religion designated by an attitude. Because *Islam* means "acceptance" and even "acceptance in peace." That's what *as-salaamu alaykum* means: "Peace be with you." In other words, the acceptance of the will of God.

- **Isn't this a point that all religions have in common?**

Yes, and that's why, to return to the symbol of the wheel, Islam, that is to say submission to God, is the axis of the wheel, the immutable center. This is shared by all religions. Doesn't Dante say, "His will is our peace"? If you are in the center of the wheel in submission to the Divine, you are in Truth, whether you are Christian, Muslim, Buddhist, or whatever. It's in this sense that so many spiritual guides affirm that all people who submit to the Absolute are good Muslims. Conversely, if you stay on the rim of the wheel, you're like the fanatic mullahs or the fundamentalist Roman Catholics.

You have to reach the center of this yielding to the Divine, and when you arrive at the ultimate center, you also find the other souls, each according to their tradition.

- **It's totally ecumenical.**

Yes. In the center of the wheel there can be no fanaticism. You cannot have the intolerable pretension of being the only one to possess the truth.

- **In my church, they often presented God like a father. A fair father, but strict. It took me a long time to discover that God was also a mother. How is God presented to young Muslims?**

For Muslims, God can neither be a father nor a mother. I even believe that it would be a sacrilege to see in God a father like the Christians or a mother like the Hindus. When we think of God, we think of the Absolute. We customarily translate *La ilaha illa Allah*, the phrase that is sufficient for you to become a Muslim, by "There is no god but God." That translation is a little simplistic. In all rigor, we should translate it as "There is no reality other than Reality." In other words, everything relative is established by an Absolute.

This doesn't necessarily make things simple for Muslims. We could say, for example, that Christianity is a bridge that goes from the human condition to the divine. So we can take this bridge. In Islam, there isn't a bridge. The individual is "alone before the

Alone" to use a phrase from Plotinus.[7] The individual is certainly within a community but alone before Divine Spirit with the Qur'an as nourishment. There is no possible anthropomorphism, which explains the prohibition of statues and images. My orthodox friends are always shocked when I tell them that I am not touched by icons. I find them very beautiful, but I just can't go there.

- **You said earlier that the New Testament is inspired, while the Qur'an and the Torah are revealed. I would like you to go back to this distinction.**

In the Torah and the Qur'an, you can't change a letter. It's in this sense that they have been dictated, or if you prefer, revealed.

When I studied the scriptures, I was constantly struck by the fact that other than the last Gospel (John), the three others known as the Synoptic Gospels reported the same words in totally different circumstances. How could this be? The Bible scholars of Tubingen concluded that there must have been, in the early days of the church, collections of verses from Jesus, anthologies used for catechism. Later, once the eye witnesses were dead, they just couldn't remember exactly. It was at that point that they began to try to establish a core text, and that explains why the Gospels were written so late.

One of these anthologies was discovered in the mid-20th century in Egypt. I'm very aware of it because I was in Cairo at the time working for the French National Center for Scientific Research (CNRS).

In 1947, some British tourists traveling in the desert near Cairo panicked when they saw villagers burning sheets of parchment to make tea. They jumped up, pulled them from the flames and realized later that they were the words (sayings, utterances) of Jesus, reported in Coptic [the former Egyptian language], without any accompanying context. This anthology was rather quickly christened the fifth Gospel or the Gospel according to Thomas.

These were sheets of parchment tied up by string, like the

---

7. Plotinus (c. 204/5–270). Philosopher in the Greek tradition, born in Egypt, father of Neoplatonism. He had great influence on religions and philosophy of the region, including the ancient world, Judaism, Christianity, Islam, through the Renaissance and into the modern age. In the 20th century in India, his works are compared by Coomaraswamy to the Hindi Advaita Vedanta (non-duality/unity) philosophy, developed in approximately the same era as Plotinus.

portfolios of traders in the olden days. They were stored in large jars in the homes of cenobite monks[8] who must have left Jerusalem after its destruction in the year 70 C.E.[9] These papers were, in a way, the library of monks living in the middle of the desert, in a climate so dry that the texts were perfectly conserved.

I held these sheets of parchment in my hands and I, along with Henri Peuch,[10] my former professor from the Collège de France, presented the first summary report for the French Académie des Inscriptions et Belles-Lettres.[11] It was fascinating.

According to the accounts, there were 214 or 216 *logia*, that is, words of Christ. Two hundred and twelve of them are found in the synoptic Gospels, just as they were and without context. Two had been discovered in the proceedings from the trials of the Cathars[12] and two were on a piece of parchment used to wrap fish later purchased by St. Augustine in Ostia.[13] Just like a police thriller!

You can easily see here the difference between an inspired book and a revealed book. With the exception of this Coptic text, which is only a collection of sayings, the Gospels are biographies.

---

8. Cenobitic monasticism, unlike hermits, involves solitary time, as well as time in community with others (usual meals and rituals are shared in community, though not always involving conversation). From the Greek word for shared or common and the Latin word for life.

9. C.E., Common Era. Modern usage, removing attachments to any specific religion.

10. Henri-Charles Peuch (1902–1986). French professor, trained in philosophy, especially Greek philosophers, but later focused on the early Christian era. For twenty years he served as the Chair of Religious Studies at the prestigious Collège de France, introducing many people to the positive and fascinating qualities of non-European religions. His research caused him to be a valued contributor in analyzing and translating what later was called the Gospel of Thomas, written on pieces of parchment rediscovered in Egyptian caves by local Bedouins.

11. "In the words of the Académie's charter, it is primarily concerned with the study of the monuments, the documents, the languages, and the cultures of the civilizations of antiquity, the Middle Ages, and the classical period, as well as those of non-European civilizations."

12. Cathars, French Gnostic movement. Its followers were declared heretics, leading to a massacre of some twenty thousand people in the 13th century.

13. Ostia, harbor of ancient Rome the mouth of the Tiber River.

III

- **What strikes me is that the words from what is called the Gospel of Thomas are relatively esoteric, in any case difficult to understand.**

That's true, but you can find almost all of them in the Synoptic Gospels.

- **I wonder if they are accessible to ordinary mortals.**

Do you believe that Jesus would be accessible to ordinary mortals if we didn't reduce him to a simple message of love and peace?

- **But the circumstances surrounding the words make them easier to understand.**

No doubt. As to the Qur'an, I certainly saw something very curious that clearly shows how it was dictated. I believe I already mentioned that the Prophet was illiterate and that he necessarily should have been, because he had to be intellectually as virgin as the Virgin Mary was physically.

I lived in Cairo with adorable Sufi friends. Those five years there were without a doubt the happiest of my life. The sheikh of my friend was at the same time the guardian of a mysterious treasure hidden in a mosque in Cairo. In this mosque there was a door that aroused everyone's curiosity. It had a window, but the window was hidden behind a brass panel that was only opened, they said, for very important dignitaries. I was far from being a dignitary, but thanks to the sheikh, my friend was able to get me in. I was stupefied to see there one of the first dictations of the Qur'an. Imagine a cubic meter of gazelle hides. On these hides was written, with a stylus, what the Prophet dictated at the very moment when he received it. People believe that the scribe was Ali, but they are not totally sure. These pieces of gazelle hide are different sizes and they look like a gigantic puzzle. We brought with us a Tunisian student who burst into tears on seeing this. It was very strange. The pieces were not in any order. You had the impression of someone who had written a telephone number on the back of an envelope or on a scrap of paper. The Prophet just said what was dictated to him at that very moment. Only later was it put in order.

- **Could you read it?**

No, because I don't know Arabic well enough.

I also saw the Qur'an of Osman (Uthman)[14] in Istanbul. This one is very touching because there is a trace of blood on one of the pages. Uthman was stabbed while he was reading it. There are still many people who know the Qur'an by heart. It's difficult because there are many verses that are very similar. Although transcribed during the Prophet's lifetime, under Uthman's direction, the Qur'an was later established as a book in the form we have today.

- **So Muhammad was merely a channel through which the word of God passed?**

Exactly, and that is why Muslims do not worship him. He did not have a double nature, as Christians believe Jesus does. Look at Jesus. Sometimes he speaks like a man and sometimes like God. In the Hellenistic world, the idea that a man could have a double nature, divine and human, was not unthinkable. In a Semitic context, like the Arab context, it was unthinkable. The Jews never deified Moses. No more than the Muslims deified Muhammad.

If you read the sayings (hadith) of the Prophet carefully, you notice there are two sorts of prophetic utterances: The first kind, where Muhammad speaks like a man when they ask him, for example, how to pray or make the ablutions; and the other kind, when he pronounced divinely inspired words.[15] For example, "I was a hidden treasure and I wished to be known. That is why I created the world." Or again, "I only created people to worship me." What's curious is that when he pronounced these inspired words, no one was ever tempted to attribute them to him. People who were hostile to him said he was an imposter, but it never crossed their mind to say that he passed himself off as God. You are right: He was merely a channel.

- **I am often struck by the double language of the Gospels. Christ sometimes presents himself as a man and sometimes as God.**

He never really presents himself as God. When they ask him if he is

---

14. Uthman ibn Affan in Arabic, or Osman in Turkish and Persian (579–656). Companion of the Prophet, later Caliph, 644-656, who assembled the verses of the Qur'an into the authorized version of the text.

15. While these short verses are not part of the Qur'an, they are called sacred or holy sayings (hadith *qudsi*), sacred utterances, and Muslims consider them to be revealed by God through Muhammad.

the Messiah, he answers, "You said this." Chouraqui says that it's a misunderstanding and that it means, "It's you who says that. Not I."

- **Some believe that there is confusion between the historical Jesus and the universal Christ and that this confusion is the basis of many problems. They are very willing to see Christ as a man who, little by little, was filled with God, to the point of becoming divine. Then all the contradictions are explained and resolve themselves.**

A man totally realized as Jesus was, can only be the Great Self. It's in this sense that al-Hallaj said, "I am God." He wanted to say that he was so filled with the Divine that his own life no longer existed.

- **Can't we also say that it's perhaps a matter of an intense nostalgia: the memory of a state that we once knew and that we want to rediscover?**

You know, the *Mathnawi* begins with a really nostalgic song, "Listen to the reed flute," in which Rumi complains about the separation:

Since I was cut from the reed bed of my birth
I want to be reunited with it
My heart is torn by thirst
And by nostalgia.

You asked me how the book of Iqbal was able to trigger such a change in me. I would say that it was a reminder. For me, the discovery of Islam was like finding something again.

The only country where I feel at home is not Paris, where I am merely a dazzled tourist. It isn't Greece either, where I am nonetheless like a fish in water because I love both the Classical Greek thinkers and the people of Greece today. The only country where I really feel at home is in Turkey. When I arrive, I am like a cat who has found its own home again. I recognize the smells, and people stop me on the street to ask me for directions. They think I'm Turkish and I look like an idiot when I answer them. I really feel like I'm in my own country.

- **In Konya or in all of Turkey?**

In all of Turkey, and more in Konya than elsewhere. There's a sort of atmosphere there. Something happened to me that was really strange, even if it doesn't prove anything. One of my Egyptian friends took me one day to a spiritual clairvoyant. She was a villager, completely illiterate. As soon as I arrived, she regarded me with a strange look. I couldn't speak Arabic very well but we could understand each other because she knew some English words. I wrote down everything she said, which was about like this:

> Oh how strange! I can see you in a country where there are no cars, no trains, no planes, nothing but horses and mules. I see you walking. You are walking long distances on foot. Wow! You really are walking. And what strange names there are in this country! Wait, I see Ko ... Ko ... Ko ...

I asked her if it weren't Konya and she cried, "Yes! That's it! I see you sitting next to a spiritual guide and what's strange is that you are writing down his words. You are still writing them today, but it's in another language."

We went to see this woman a little for amusement, but you must admit, I had every reason to be surprised. I can agree with you that this doesn't prove anything. It's perhaps just a dip into the collective subconscious, something we can't understand, but it's certainly curious.

- **Isn't it especially curious that you had the impression from the beginning of being at home in Konya and with Islam?**

I hesitate to say what I'm going to tell you now because I may give the impression of being vain about it, when I'm not. I studied Persian, but I don't understand it as well as French or English. Well, in Konya or Ankara or Istanbul I often have to make microfilms of Rumi texts. This is not always easy because there are sometimes holes in the manuscript. It's okay when we can reestablish the meaning from the context, but that's not always the case. To give you an example, we can read, "The Master dreamed of ..." and there's a completely illegible word there. The Master could have dreamed about anything, flowers, angels, fish ... Impossible to know. In cases like this, I have often sought counsel from Iranians, professors, or specialists on Rumi. Well, when they gave me their explanation, often I didn't agree. I didn't really know why but that's just how it was. Sometimes my friends made a little fun of me. They said that I had a lot of nerve and that, after all, I don't speak Persian as well as they do. I insisted, however, and often I have seen them come back to me later to tell me, "You were the one who was right. We found a manuscript that proved it."

One day one of my friends told me, "It's curious, you don't master Persian exceptionally well, but you have in you some sort of divining ability." She was right. Often when they gave me a new manuscript and there a doubtful word, I was able to guess it. I had the impression that I had always known it.

- **We could ask if this doesn't come from another life.**

Who knows?

- **That would be amazing if you had been a disciple of Rumi's sitting at his feet . . .**

When I took my first steps towards Islam, after reading the book by Iqbal, you can imagine that it was not easy. I had been brought up in the Catholic religion by a grandmother who was originally Anglican. I had a Jewish husband. I had the feeling of doing something crazy and I was sometimes even more lost because I had no one to guide me. Sometimes I asked in my prayers, "Tell me what I should do. Give me a sign."

I received this sign in the form of a dream. I dreamed that I was buried and somehow was able to see my tomb, a tomb like I had never seen before, and on it was my name, Eva, which is pronounced Hawa, [also spelled *Hawwa*], written in the Arabic letters also used for Persian. This seemed very strange to me and, even as I slept, I said to myself, "But after all, I'm not dead." To convince myself even more, I wiggled my toes.

When I woke up, I remembered saying to myself, "Well, my dear girl, you asked for a sign and you got one: You will be buried as a Muslim."

I forgot about this dream and continued along my path to Islam very naturally. Fifteen years later, I took my first trip to Istanbul. I met one of the whirling dervishes that I had invited to perform at the Théâtre de la Ville several years earlier in conjunction with UNESCO. He was an architect by training, because dervishes, as you probably know, far from being monks, lead a normal life with families and jobs. This friend said to me, "You who are so interested in Rumi, you should come and see the work that I'm in charge of in a very old house for Sufi retreats that is now a museum." I went there and had to walk over rubble, dirt, and rusted metal. My friend took my hand and we clambered along. The main gate was broken and way at the back there was a sort of little pavilion that workers were in the process of restoring. I was a little nervous, I admit, trying not to ruin my stockings or sprain an ankle, when suddenly, my heart stopped beating. Right in front of me, I saw the tombstone I had dreamed about, exactly the same, except that my name wasn't engraved on it.

I asked the architect, "What is this strange tombstone?" and he answered that it was a woman's tombstone. "What we're clearing out here," he said, "is the cemetery of women who were disciples of Rumi during his lifetime and who wanted to be buried here. This cemetery was later abandoned for centuries. We are going to bulldoze it and plant flowers in its place."

Several years later, this name Hawa that I saw on the tomb very officially became my own. When I wanted to make the pilgrimage to Mecca, I went to get the authorization from Al-Azhar University. I came across a sheikh I knew and he asked me, "What's your name in Islam?" I answered that I didn't have a Muslim name and he said I absolutely had to have one. I was so self-taught that I didn't even know that. I was embarrassed and he found the solution. "All you have to do," he said, "is take the Islamic version of your name, Eva. After all, it's a name from the Qur'an." So that's how I became Hawa, the same name I saw in my dream on my tombstone.

You see, everything seemed to come together to make me a Muslim. Even in the beginning, I had the feeling that I knew the customs of Islam without having learned them. There was one, for example, of never throwing a paper on which the name of God is written into a trash can. To get rid of it, you must burn it. When I became a Muslim, I did that without knowing why. Later I learned it was the recommended practice.

Indeed, on this topic there is a very lovely Sufi story. It's the story of a very bad person who spent all his time drinking and running around. He was really the shame and scandal of the neighborhood. One day when he was walking across the marketplace, half drunk, he saw a piece of paper on the ground with the name of God written on it. He picked it up and saw that it was covered with mud. This upset him greatly and, when he got home, he did everything he could to clean it. Because he didn't have any water, he rubbed it with a piece of musk that he had picked up. The next night, he had a dream during which God said to him, "You have perfumed my name, so I will perfume your heart." Later, this drunken derelict became a great saint.

Long before I knew this story, I instinctively couldn't throw away a paper or a newspaper on which the name of God was written. And it was the same for everything. I knew what to do as if I had been brought up in Islam. I remember one day, after a conference, some monks came to see me to say, "You who know the Christian mystics so well, why did you choose Islam?" I could only answer, "I don't know, but I know that I couldn't be anywhere else."

- **Isn't it difficult to adapt to the rituals of a new religion?**

But you know, in Islam the rituals are reduced to the minimum. I didn't even need to record my conversion. All you have to do is say sincerely before God, "I affirm with all my heart and with all my mind that there is no other divinity than the Divine."[16]

- **Any believer can say that, whatever his or her tradition.**

That's true, but you should really add, "I affirm that Muhammad is his Prophet." I must emphasize the fact that there is no question of worshiping Muhammad. By recognizing him as a prophet, you recognize all the others, because he is their successor.

- **So Islam also recognizes Jesus?**

Yes, but as a prophet, not as the only son of God. Therein lies the great point of contention between Christianity and Islam.

- **It's really a shame that so many men and women have been killed for this point of doctrine.**

I am of the same opinion as you. I admit that in recognizing Muhammad as a prophet, I did not have the impression of denying anything. I can continue to believe in the mission of Jesus and the Virgin Mary. I simply had the feeling of setting aside what some would call the "the theological mumbo jumbo."

---

16. The Islamic credo, "There is no god but God." (Arabic, "*La illaha illa Allah.*")

- **What do you mean by that?**

This way that theologians spend their time splitting hairs, end-lessly discussing the relationship between the three members of the Trinity. All this exasperated me to such a point. But how could you expect me to deny the message of Christ? I cannot.

Indeed, if you are sincere, you don't even need to convert. Any believer can be a Muslim in the large sense of the spiritual attitude. All he or she has to do is to submit to God's will. This submission, this surrender of themselves to the divine will, isn't this the central axis common to all religions?

- **Any Christian can say the first part of the conversion expression but certainly not the second.**

No, because that would necessarily imply that the message brought by Muhammad is an authentic message: a message that does not admit that Jesus was the only son of God, because in the eyes of Islam, God cannot have a son. But as a Muslim, I can consider that Jesus is a person completely inhabited by the Divine. Even if he is not God, the Absolute, the creator of the galaxies, he is nonetheless completely filled with the Divine Spirit.

You know, if there is a difference in dogma between Christians and Muslims, there are also misunderstandings in language over the centuries. This is very important. I'd like to return to this famous expression *Mother of God*, because, when I was Christian, I said it without knowing what I was saying. If that means the Mother of Jesus or even Mother of Christ, yes, why not? But if that means the Mother of the Absolute, the Mother of the Creator, well that's something else entirely.

Take the expression *Son of God*. They tell us he's a person in the Trinity, but what should we understand by this word *person*? We can discuss this forever. A person is an individual, a separate being, quite distinct from other individuals. Should we talk about separate persons or attributes of the same God?

- **In the same way that you say "In the Name of God, the Merciful and the Compassionate."**

Exactly. These qualities are the attributes of the same God. But talking about persons, that means talking about different entities, and Muslims cannot admit that. Just as they cannot accept, in the

Apostles' Creed, that Jesus is "seated at the right hand of God the Father Almighty." When you are on the right of someone, even if you take it symbolically, you are separate from the person beside whom you are seated, and therefore distinct from them.

The whole problem is there. Everything depends on the meaning you give to the word *person*. I can recognize you as Jean-Pierre, as a writer, and as my friend. These are attributes of your person. This doesn't mean that you are three men. If you say in Arabic, three persons, this means three people. Sometimes I talk with my Muslim friends and defend this vision of the Trinity, but they immediately say, "Have you seen the façade of the church at Vézelay?[17] There's God the Father, God the Son, and God the Holy Spirit. And look at some of the miniatures from the Middle Ages, you see God with a beard and a crown holding on his knees the baby God who is holding against his breast a dove representing God the Holy Spirit."

- **There is the icon of Rublev.[18]**

Yes, but it's certainly anthropomorphism.

- **But it's not important.**

It's very important because it widens the gap.

- **Yes, but the most important thing is that a Sufi, a Christian monk, or a Tibetan lama have, in different forms, the same experience of God. There can't be two experiences of God.**

Of course, but language that separates is language separating needlessly.

- **It's simply needless language.**

If you will, but when you say "There is no god but God," that doesn't introduce error. You can't stop an individual from a non-Christian tradition from understanding it means three gods when you speak of three enduring manifestations of God. When you say that Jesus is at the right hand of God, where he will judge the living and the

---

17. Vézelay Abbey was a pilgrimage site during the Middle Ages, and even today. The elaborate façade is covered with statuary. The site is said to house remains of Mary Magdalene.

18. Andrei Rublev (ca.1370–1430). One of Russia's greatest painters of icons.

dead, it means that he is distinct from his Father. It at least creates a duality.

And then, I have to admit, the presumptuousness of some theologians sometimes exasperates me. When we don't really even know what a lump of sugar or a piece of bread is, they have interminable discussions about the relationship that exists between the three persons in the Trinity.

- **But all this would disappear if you consider the Trinity as three aspects, three attributes of the same God.**

Of course, but the language is very misleading because "a person" is not a single attribute. If I say Rachel is a nice person, that doesn't mean that she has only one attribute. I believe there's a fundamental misunderstanding here.

- **And did you believe it from the beginning? Everything you just said, did you feel it very deeply as soon as you discovered Islam?**

I already felt it before. I frequently read St. John of the Cross and he is very influenced by Arab thought and I found myself in his "Nothingness, nothingness," which is a really negative theology. But I remain frightened by the constant risk of anthropomorphism. Obviously Islam has the opposite difficulty because the individual is alone before God. "Alone before the Alone," as Plotinus says. You have nothing to hang on to and this solitude before the Absolute can sometimes be hard to bear.

- **But don't people attach themselves a little to Muhammad?**

Not really, because it is forbidden to pray to him. Indeed it is also forbidden to pray to saints. You can pray *for* the saints or even for the Prophet. The thinking is that even if the Prophet is a holy man, he is infinitely far from being as holy as God.

- **Still, can't we ask him to help us for this or that?**

No doubt in practice people do that. There is superstition everywhere. In the ritual prayer, you can pray for the Prophet, "O Lord, bless your servant Muhammad," but never, ever, *to* the Prophet. The holiness of God is so inconceivable that a man, however holy he may be, doesn't come close. In orthodox Islam there are no intermediaries.

- **You speak with such a peace of mind, it is calming to be near you. Still, you must have had some doubts and even struggles when you first converted to Islam.**

I told you, I took three years to study the Bible to decide with full knowledge.

I even went to see a bishop. One day, Louis Massignon, whom I consider my spiritual guide, said to me, "If this is your path, I fully support your converting to Islam, but I would still like you to talk to my friend, the bishop of Strasbourg, before you take this step."

Everything Massignon told me was like gospel for me, so I went to see his friend. I went all the more readily because he [the bishop] was in favor of a reconciliation between the Anglicans and the Roman Catholics. This touched me personally because my beloved grandmother was originally Anglican.

So here I was in front of this bishop who welcomed me warmly. He listened to me attentively, then said, "I honestly understand that you can't remain a Catholic, but because your grandmother was an Anglican, why not become a Protestant? It's still less of a change than becoming a Muslim."

I responded with a cry from the heart, you know, those things you say because they pop out of you and they express exactly your most profound thought. So I exclaimed, "But Monsignor, that would be too easy!" He looked at me a long time and said, "I understand. You are right. Do what you want." That was thirty years ago.

I asked myself later why I pronounced that unexpected phrase. Why would it have been easier for me to become a Protestant? In becoming a Protestant, I would be giving myself the right to choose, which was very important in my eyes, but at the same time, I would be giving myself the feeling of sampling here and there, of taking what pleased me and leaving the rest. So becoming a Muslim was really a commitment of my whole being.

- **This must have been a shock for those you loved, for your husband and your parents.**

Not especially for my husband. He was indifferent, but he knew how to respect the difference. It was a little as if I had just said that I was going to learn Chinese. My father was still alive, but religious questions were not very important to him. On the other hand, I lost some friends, no doubt those who didn't love me that much. Fortunately for me, the others remained faithful.

- **If someone came to see you and said they wanted to convert to Islam, would you encourage them?**

Not necessarily. It depends. Some time ago, I met with a young man coming back from Yemen where he had been a volunteer.[19] He said, "Madam, I have come to see you because I attended one of your conferences. I love the Arab world. I, who was brought up in the banking circles of an elegant Parisian neighborhood, was welcomed in Yemen in a simple tent." He spoke of the starry sky, the silence of the desert, the hospitality, and finished by saying, "Naturally I want to become a Muslim. What do you think?"

"Because you are asking me, I would strongly discourage you."

"You, of all people, are telling me this?"

"Yes. Granted, the Yemenis are charming, they play beautiful music under starry skies, but that's not enough. Entering Islam means a long period of self-discipline. You have to prepare yourself first."

This word *conversion* that we use every which way, I don't like it at all. Especially as there are as many paths as there are individuals. For some, it's a thunderbolt, for others, the journey is two steps forward and one step backward, as it was for me for a long time.

I have very good friends, for example, who experienced the thunderbolt. When they arrived in Cairo, they went into a mosque and they felt like the ceiling fell on their head. Even today, they are incapable of saying why they, both of them together, burst into tears. They became fervent Muslims.

Other friends experienced a more arduous journey, often even frankly difficult.

Indeed the path doesn't matter. The essential is to get to the end.

---

19. In lieu of French military service, compulsory for all males at that time.

IV

- Now we've been talking a long time and we're surprised to note that your beloved Rumi's name has only come up rarely in our conversation. He nonetheless played a major role in your path to Islam and your interior life. How did you discover him?

When I read the book by Iqbal that we've talked so much about, I was intrigued to see him endlessly quoting his spiritual guide, Jalaluddin Rumi. I had never even heard of this name and I said to myself over and over, "But who is this man?" I immediately went to the Bibliothèque Nationale,[1] to the National School of Oriental Languages, and to specialized libraries. I learned that he was a mystic from the 13th century, but it was difficult for me to learn much more because there had been no translations of his works into French. I discovered some texts in English translated by Nicholson and some poems translated into German. Nothing else, but what I read seemed so exquisite that I decided to get a diploma in Persian in order to make these treasures known to the West. After three years of study, I could get down to work.

The more I advanced, the more I was stupefied by what I discovered. Rumi lived in the 13th century. In other words, he was a contemporary of St. Francis of Assisi,[2] whom he resembled in many respects, by his love of poetry, of nature, of animals, and of poor people. He was seen in a bad light by publicly "correct" people because he spent time consoling prostitutes. He said that his only task was to awaken souls that were asleep. His immense poetic oeuvre had no other purpose. Without a doubt his greatest

---

1. The French national library.
2. Francis of Assisi (1181/1182–1226). Italian friar, author, preacher, and founder of several religious orders for men and for women. He traveled to Egypt to try to put an end to the Crusades. Canonized two years after his death by Pope Gregory IX, St. Francis and St. Catherine of Siena (1347–1380) are considered the patron saints of Italy. St. Francis is also associated with the environment and kindness to animals.

work, which I recently completed translating, is the *Mathnawi*, a universe unto itself.

He was also a great thinker. Imagine, in the middle of the 13th century, he thought that if we split the atom, we would find a core with planets revolving around it. Indeed he also had an insight about the extraordinary energy contained in atoms, announcing that we should be very careful about provoking a shock that could reduce the world to ashes. He also talked at length about evolution.

What's even more extraordinary, and what struck me personally, is that he said, "On this little planet Earth, which is only a little corner of the universe," (and not at all its center as they believed in the Middle Ages), "all human beings are subject to the influence of the stars. The moon affects the fertility of women and the tides, while the sun acts on vegetation."

- **We already, even during his era, had a good idea about the influence of the moon.**

Yes, but he adds, and I translate this literally from Persian, "What we realize less, is that the smallest gesture of a person on this planet is perceived in solar systems belonging to galaxies not yet discovered."

When I translated this, I pinched myself to see if I were not dreaming and I remembered that one day, when I was having coffee in Fez with Olivier Costa de Beauregard,[3] he asked me, "You know, my dear friend, we physicists on the cutting edge, if we tell the public what we are discovering, they would consider us crazy. For example, if you touch your coffee cup, Einstein confirms that your gesture is perceived in other solar systems." My heart skipped a beat when I remembered that Rumi had said the same thing in the 13th century.

- **You were so enthusiastic that you have devoted a great deal of your life to translating his works.**

Indeed, I believe I have translated just about everything. The publication of the *Mathnawi* is a big event for me.

---

3. Olivier Costa de Beauregard (1911-2007). French quantum physicist as well as a philosopher of science. He was also recognized for his work on time and information theory.

IV

- Perhaps we're being a little indiscreet, but we would
  like to have a better sense of the relationship you have
  with him.

It's a bit like the relationship between a disciple and a spiritual guide.
He is of such stature, of such dimension, his message is so great!

- But a spiritual guide, you talk to him, you ask him
  for advice, for direction. Can you really have a vital
  relationship with someone who lived so long ago?

That depends, not on the spiritual guide, but on the disciple,
indeed on the very nature of the disciple.

- Would we be going too far to say that you have dedicated your life to him?

I dedicated my life to him because I thought that his message was
so universal and so urgently needed. A message of love that brings
together the most essential values of Christianity and Islam without denying anything, and gives them a totally fraternal and ecumenical dimension. You cannot find in him the least bit of dogma-
tism, and that seems to me enormously important.

- Don't you feel a little like an orphan, now that you
  have finished the translation of his works?

After this birth, I think I will start over rereading it with another
set of eyes. Not those of the translator.
    You know, when you do a translation that is really rather diffi-
cult, you stick to the text, you constantly ask if this word is or isn't
the right word. I am happy now to be able to step back a little and
look at him with a different perspective.

- The perspective of the disciple rather than the translator?

Exactly.

- We don't mean to tell his entire life story here in detail.
  We do, however, need some biographical notes, just
  enough to know what struck you the most about him.

He was born in Balkh in Afghanistan. His father [Bahauddin Valad]
was a theologian, so famous that they named him the "Sultan of
Scholars." He too had an extraordinary gift of foresight because

following a revelation, he left Balkh with his family just before the city was completely destroyed by the Mongols.

So they set out as wanderers, which first led them to Nishapur where they met the famous poet, Attar, whom Rumi soon considered one of his spiritual guides.

After living in Mecca, they arrived in Turkey and stopped in Konya, which was called Iconium in the time of St. Paul. When they arrived, it was ruled by a philanthropic Seljuk sultan who was very open and very liberal. A friend of the sciences and the arts, he had prevented the destruction of numerous sculptures from antiquity that you can still see today. On learning that the traveler who had just arrived in his town was a great scholar, he invited him to continue his work preaching in Konya and even gave him a college where he taught until his death. Naturally, Rumi automatically followed in his father's footsteps.

- **Was he already a great mystic?**

Not yet. At the time he was more of a very scholarly lawyer, and, at the same time, of course, a very pious, very spiritual man. We know that he had many students.

At the age of seven, however, he had already had an extraordinary premonition that Aflaki[4] tells us about. When he was saying his morning prayers, he read the al-Kawthar chapter of the Qur'an that begins with these words: "We have granted to thee the fount of Abundance . . ."

"I cried," he later said, "when God in His infinite compassion, revealed Himself to me, in a way that caused me to faint. When I came back to my senses, I heard a mysterious voice saying to me, 'O Jalaluddin! By the authority of our splendor, I command you not to struggle in the future, because we have made you a place of contemplation.'"

From this unheard-of experience, Rumi later drew this conclusion: "In thanks for this favor, I served others to the limit and I tried to live up to these words from the Qur'an, 'So would I not be a grateful servant?'[5] in hopes of enabling my companions to

---

4. Shams ud-Din Ahmad Aflaki (ca.1286-1291). Dervish and disciple of Rumi's grandson, as well as biographer-hagiographer of texts about the virtues of Rumi and his disciples.
5. The phrase "grateful servant" is an allusion to (at least) two verses about the relationship between the Divine and the human. The Arabic word 'abd is

reach the perfection of ecstasy."

- **So from his childhood he was a true mystic?**

No doubt he had been touched by the ecstasy, but the great revelation, the one that changed his life, dates from his encounter with Shams Tabrizi.

One day when he was leaving his college, riding on a mule and surrounded by many students, he was stopped by a wandering dervish, a certain Shams from the area of Tabriz [in present day Iran], who whispered a question in his ear. The question was so extraordinary that Rumi got down from his mule and took Shams by the hand and dragged him behind him. The two men went away for a long retreat during which . . .

- **You didn't tell us what the question was.**

We don't know. There are many hypotheses, but no certainty. Undoubtedly it was about something really mystical. In any event, after he returned from the retreat, Rumi pronounced this famous sentence:

"My life is contained in three words: I was raw, I was cooked, and finally charred."

This image was later used by Meister Eckhart[6] and Simone Weil.[7] It is true that authentic mystics experience the same blazing intuition, the same transmutation of the soul in a crucible. Indeed, it was in this very moment Rumi really grasped the extent of divine love.

- **Couldn't we say that it was at this moment that he settled into divine love?**

If you like. This very scholarly man became the humble disciple

---

usually translated as "servant" or "slave," but it comes from the root meaning "to worship," hence the name *Abdullah* (originally used by Jews, Christians, and Muslims), also means "the worshiper of God," and does not describe a demeaning relationship.

6. Johannes Eckhart also called Meister (Master) Eckhart (around 1260-1328), 13th century German Dominican friar, theologian, philosopher, and mystic. His works are admired by modern mystics and philosophers, especially those who espouse non-duality.

7. Simone Weil (1909-1943). French mystic, philosopher, and social activist who joined the French Resistance. Although Jewish, her mystical writings are primarily about her spiritual connection with Jesus Christ.

of a wandering dervish that no one had ever heard of. They lived together a long time, which didn't please the other disciples of Rumi at all and they repeated to him endlessly, "After all, you are handsome, elegant, well-read, cultivated, you are a great spiritual guide. Why are you like a puppy before this unshaven and untidy man?" Shams suffered from this hostility. One day he was tired of it all and, without telling anyone, he left for Damascus.

Rumi became so desperate that his son, Sultan Valad, went immediately to Damascus to bring back Shams on his horse while Sultan Valad walked on foot beside him.

Life returned to what it had been before, but alas, not for long, because one day Shams disappeared. He vanished into thin air and no one ever found a trace of him. We have every reason to believe that he was assassinated by the disciples of Rumi.

Needless to say, Rumi was inconsolable. On the door of the room where Shams, whose name means "Sun," had lived, he wrote this short poem:

> I was snow, in your rays I melted;
> The earth drank me; as mist of spirit
> I rise again towards the sun.

Finally one day, Rumi realized that his spiritual guide was alive in him and would never be separated from him, and then he came out of his depression.

- **You said we have every reason to believe that Shams had been assassinated. On what do you base this statement?**

It's a long story, and sometimes so strange that I hesitate to tell it.

First I have to tell you about the mosque of Shams in Konya. It's not that it's especially pretty. Indeed, it is not from that period. But in this mosque, where there is an empty catafalque,[8] strange things happen.

The first time I went inside, in 1969, I felt horribly bad, as if I might faint. I didn't understand why. As I am quite practical, I said to myself, "It's just because I haven't had my breakfast yet." Once I was outside, I was surprised to feel perfectly fine. I went back in several times, and on each occasion, the malaise came back.

---

8. A box or platform on which a body or casket is placed during a funeral.

Returning to my hotel, I met the dervishes that I knew and one of them asked me, "Where are you coming from with this ghastly complexion?" I explained what I had just been through and he did not seem surprised. "Ah," he said, "that's something that happens frequently." He didn't want to tell me anything else.

A second story, just as curious, happened about six years ago. One day I received a phone call from Father Poncet, a well-traveled, outspoken Dominican priest who knows Turkey like the back of his hand, who even organizes trips to Turkey for La Procure.[9]

"My dear friend," he said to me, "I am really embarrassed: I was supposed to leave the day after tomorrow for Konya, but I can't move. I have a 104-degree fever and no one can replace me. Would you please take my place? You won't have to act as a guide at all because there is already one coming. All that I ask is that, in the evening, you go over the events of the day with the group, mainly composed of university people."

I accepted immediately and went off with a very nice group of university people, mainly agnostics, except for one Catholic couple who, at first, seemed a little traditional to me. It was beautiful weather when we arrived in front of the mosque of Shams. There was not a leaf moving on a tree. We went into the mosque and, suddenly, we were in a whirlwind, a little like the mistral wind in the south of France, whipping along Marseille's Canebière Street. We swayed back and forth, holding onto each other and were barely able to remain standing. It was really frightening, because there wasn't a single window open. I looked out the window and saw that the trees were perfectly still.

A few years later I received a phone call from one of my good friends who had been the conservator of the Rumi museum and who had become the Minister of Culture in Turkey. "You know," he said to me, "we have found the body of Shams. We were working in the mosque and, while digging rather deep, we discovered a skeleton that can only be his." I remembered the unbelievable whirlwind that threw us against one another over the very place where they found the skeleton.

You know, there are places that are charged with spiritual energy without our knowing quite why. The well that's inside

---

9. La Procure is one of the largest chains of religious bookstores in Europe, founded in France in 1898, associated with the Roman Catholic Church. It also includes social and cultural gatherings for authors and supporters.

Chartres Cathedral,[10] for example. The place where the Maharishi[11] lived, Sainte-Baume,[12] and so on. For people who are rather sensitive, like me, it is sometimes difficult to go there.

- **The fact that his skeleton was discovered doesn't tell us one way or the other whether Shams was assassinated.**

No, but I have another curious story to tell you about this subject.

Several years ago, I was walking in Konya, with my hands in my pockets like a real tourist. I was window-shopping, trying to decide what gifts to bring to my friends when, in an area about the size of this room, I felt very, very bad. As I am hypoglycemic, I was afraid I'd faint, but once I left that place, I felt fine again. Just to be sure, I walked back and had the same discomfort.

A little while later, this same friend, the [Turkish] minister of culture, said to me, "You know we are now almost certain about the place where Shams was trapped and then murdered." He described the place, not far from the market, and it was exactly where I had felt so bad.

When you stop to think about it, that's not really surprising. I believe that some things remain and certain tragic events mark the places where they occur. I could cite several other examples like this, and I am not the only one who could.

- **Tell us about the whirling dervishes and their dance.**

Rumi created the *sama*[13] in his depression after the disappearance of Shams. It's a sacred cosmic dance, characteristic of the order he

---

10. The well at Chartres Cathedral has a reputation for healing powers. The cathedral itself is a major French site of Christian pilgrimage, and contains a tunic (*Sancta Camisa*) said to have been worn by the Virgin Mary. The tunic survived a fire that destroyed the original building in the 12th century. The current cathedral was inaugurated by King Louis IX (St. Louis).

11. Maharishi Mahesh Yogi, 20th century Indian guru and father of Transcendental Meditation.

12. Sainte-Baume (literally Holy Cave). A French tradition says that Mary Magdalene and her brother Lazarus escaped persecutions of Christians in the Holy Land by taking a small boat to France. They landed near Arles, and Lazarus went to preach the Gospel in nearby Marseille and is credited with converting the town and the region to Christianity. Mary Magdalene retired to a spiritual life of penance in a cave nearby for thirty years.

13. *Sama* (from the Arabic *sama'a*; in Turkish *sema*) literally means "listening."

founded. Later, his son, Sultan Valad,[14] codified and institutionalized it. He writes in *The Secret Word*, "The teaching of my father was
really very esoteric and very complicated. I have tried to explain it
for the general public."

- **We know people who, when they visited Turkey,
  were disappointed by the *sama*. They saw a show for
  tourists, a folk dance.**

That can be the case, unfortunately. One day, right after I first
arrived in Konya, I rushed to see a *sama*. It was in a large gym-
nasium with neon lights and there were people at the entrance
drinking cola, while others were trying to sell little brass dervish
dolls. The *sama* itself was of course beautiful, but it really wasn't
exactly what I expected. I felt a sadness in my heart and left before
the end.

On entering my room at the hotel, I was surprised to find
myself murmuring to Rumi, "Truly, I would really like to see something besides that caricature." At that very moment, the telephone
rang and they said to me, "Madam, someone is asking for you." I
said that wasn't possible, because I hadn't told anyone about my
arrival, but the receptionist insisted and said they were asking for
Dr. Eva. I then heard the voice of one of my dervish friends, "So
that's the way you walk out on us, in the middle of a *sama*?" I told
him what I had felt in my heart and he replied, "Do you believe
that it makes us happy to do folk dances? Come, we're going to do
a *sama*, just for you." So at two o'clock in the morning, I was able to
watch a *sama* that was the real cosmic dance as Rumi wanted it, the
dizzying circling of atoms and planets.

"Many paths lead to God," he said, "I chose the path of dance
and music . . . In the cadences of the music, a secret is hidden. If I
revealed it, it would radically change the world."

---

14. Sultan Valad (1226-1312). Trusted son of Jalaluddin Rumi and successor
who helped to gather and codify his father's works and practices, including the
sama, or whirling ceremony of the dervishes. Grandson of the scholar Bahauddin Valad who immigrated with his family to present-day Turkey from present-
day Afghanistan.

- **Maybe he didn't reveal the secret but he wrote a certain number of magnificent texts about the cosmic dance. Could you cite us those which touched you the most?**

There are too many. Here, listen to this poem:

> O day, arise! The atoms are dancing,
> The souls, lost in ecstasy are dancing,
> I will tell you, in your ear, where the dance leads,
> All the atoms in the air and in the desert
> You must realize they are like fools
> Each atom, happy or miserable
> Is enraptured by the ineffable Sun.

- **We'd like to hear more.**

How could the soul not take flight when, in the glorious Presence, a loving call, sweet as honey, comes right up to it and says, "Arise!"

How could the fish not jump immediately from the dry land into the water when the sound of water reaches its ear from the ocean with its cool waves?

How could the falcon not fly away, forgetting the hunt, towards the wrist of the king, as soon as it hears the jingle of his bells struck by the baton, giving it the signal to return?

How could the Sufi not begin to dance, whirling around himself like the atom, around the Eternal Sun, so he can deliver the soul from this perishable world?

Fly, fly, bird, toward your native land, because you are escaping from your cage and deploying your wings. Move away from the brackish water towards the sweet spring of life (*Diwan*).

- **Fly, bird, towards your native land. So there's something in the Sufi soul like a recollection of Paradise?**

This is a very important theme in Islamic mysticism and we will probably have occasion to return to it.

- **We don't have any difficulty understanding how marvelous you must have felt when you discovered for the first time these texts that, for eight centuries, had never been translated into most Western languages.[15]**

The word marvelous seems a little weak to me. I can even speak of stupefaction when I discovered that Rumi knew the number of planets which, in the West, wasn't known until the 20th century. The number of planets in our solar system determines the number of dancers taking part in the spiritual dance. There are always nine or a multiple of nine.

- **So the *sama* is more than a dance. Could we say it's like a liturgy?**

Absolutely, not only the *sama* dance itself, but also the music. Aflaki wrote that while Rumi was listening to an instrument he particularly liked, the call to prayer began. The friend who was with him pressured him to interrupt the concert.

"No," said the Master, "because this too is a prayer. Both are to God. He calls for the one externally for his service, and for the other internally, to love and to know."

He also said, regarding the Oriental *rebab* violin, "It's only dry string, dry wood, dry skin, but from it comes the voice of the Beloved."

Everything was a pretext for him to dance: the hammering of goldsmiths, the song of water on the mill wheel . . .. He was always on the edge of ecstasy, in this ultimate union of which he sang:

At the origin, my soul and yours were united,
They were your exterior and interior aspects and my exterior
    and interior aspects
It would be futile to say, mine and yours,
For there is neither me nor you, between me and you.

- **You could quote him for hours.**

Of course! What can I say, I lived and live in such intimacy with him. Imagine, I translated almost everything he wrote: *Odes*

---

15. Later in this text, the author speaks of the first translators into English, R.A. Nicholson and A.J. Arberry.

mystiques,[16] a book of teaching stories I entitled *Le livre du dedans*,[17] his *Quatrains*, and most especially, the fifty thousand verses of the *Mathnawi*, a vast and beautiful spiritual theodicity[18] in which you feel Rumi's immense qualities as a philosopher, a thinker, a mystic, a poet, and a commentator on the esoteric meaning of the Qur'an.

• **You emphasize his ecumenical approach a lot.**

Yes, because I think that in this regard, he is incredibly modern. Without understanding very clearly, it was what I was looking for: an ecumenical spirit that was not just syncretism,[19] because it is always easy to take a little from Islam, from Christianity, from Buddhism, or Hinduism, and make a mixture. I think the real ecumenical spirit is not at all like this and that each person should follow through to the source of his or her tradition. Then and only then, when you arrive in the middle, you find the others.

• **In the center of the wheel?**

Exactly. The wheel is the great symbol of mystics in Islam. Let's go back to this word *acceptance* to understand it better. If there is a place where all the traditions find each other, it's in acceptance. Didn't Dante say, "His will is our peace"? Many Muslims speak of "surrender to God." This fundamental attitude of abandon, of acceptance, is the immovable center of the wheel. If you stay on the circumference, you stay with those who believe they alone possess the truth and who, as a consequence, are willing to impose their will by any means. But if you go to the source of your own tradition, then you will inevitably arrive at the center of the wheel and you realize that this center is precisely the acceptance of, the surrender to the Divine. And in your acceptance, you find all the others, coming from all traditions.

---

16. *Mystical Poems of Rumi*, English translation by A.J. Arberry (1905-1969), British scholar, known for his translations of Rumi and the Qur'an.

17. *Fihi Ma Fihi*, literally, *In It What's In It*. See *Discourses of Rumi*, English translation by R.A. Nicholson (1868-1945), British scholar, known for his translations of major works of Islamic mysticism, including Rumi.

18. A spiritual poem for the Divine.

19. Syncretism is often used in a derogatory manner, as here, to describe combining beliefs and practices from different traditions.

V

• I'd like us to talk a little about Rumi's spiritual guides. There was first his father, then there was Shams Tabrizi with whom he had this mysterious relationship, but about whom we know nothing else, because he seems to have written very little and apparently had no other disciples. Besides these two, who else did Rumi consider his spiritual guides?

He said, "Attar was the soul of mysticism and Sanai was its eyes. I merely followed their footsteps."

• Who were they?

Both were marvelous poets,[1] which was no coincidence. Attar, whom Rumi met in Nishapur[2] while he was fleeing from the Mongol invasion with his father, is mainly known for his *Memorial of Saints*[3] in which he describes the lives of seventy-two saints and Sufi saints.

He also wrote the *Conference of the Birds,* which Peter Brook[4] turned into a play.

The whole story turns around a play on words: One day the birds decided to find themselves a king. They said, "All the people of the earth have a leader or a king, and we don't have one." They hold a solemn assembly and decide to go in search of the Simurgh bird and give him all power over them. *Simurgh* means "phoenix." The word play I spoke of is that in Persian the word means "thirty" (*si*) "birds" (*murgh*).

So off go our birds on the path. They cross countries and valleys, including the famous Valley of Love. Everywhere they go they

---

1. Attar and Sanai both wrote in Persian, like Rumi.
2. Located in present day Iran, Nishapur is also the birthplace of Omar Khayyam.
3. Excerpts translated as *Muslim Saints and Mystics* by A. J. Arberry.
4. Peter Brook (1925-present). British theatre director based in France, winner of multiple awards (Tonys, Grammys), for designing and directing creative productions that travel across cultures, (UK, France, USA, India, Mali).

leave some feathers, some die, and many of them become discouraged and give up. Finally, when they arrive at the threshold of the Simurgh, there are only thirty of them left.

They reach the goal after all these challenges. They meet the guardian of eternity and ask to see the Simurgh, but the guardian gives them a mirror and in the mirror, they see that they are thirty birds; that is to say, *they* are themselves this Simurgh that they so sought after. And the story ends with, "And they vanished then like the glimmer of a candle in the brightness of the sun."

All the teaching of Rumi, like that of the mystics of all times, is found in this story intended to serve as an example. The king of the birds, in other words, the goal of all spiritual quests, the One that some call God, others Allah, others the Absolute, we must find within us, in the most profound part of ourselves. And when we find the One, there is nothing else. Everything else vanishes.

• And Sanai?

Sanai was a great poet who lived about one century before Rumi. First he was a poet at the royal court and then he moved to Khorasan,[5] where he met several Sufi masters and wrote the mystical poems that are some of the most beautiful in Persian literature.

He became a spiritual guide himself, describing his path as follows:

> If you ask, O brother, what are the signs of the path, I will tell you clearly and without ambiguity. They are that you look to the truth and leave behind the false; that you turn your face toward the living world; that you rely on worthy advice; that you eliminate from your thought any ambition of glory and of reputation; that you bend your back in his service; that you purify the soul of evil and reinforce it with reason; that you leave from the home of those who speak with abundance to those who guard their silence; that you travel from the works of God to his attributes and from his attributes to his knowledge.
>
> At this moment, you go from the world of mysteries and arrive at the threshold of poverty; when you will

---

5. Khorasan is historically a Persian-speaking region which includes parts of present-day Iran, Afghanistan, Tajikistan, Uzbekistan, and Turkmenistan.

be the friend of poverty, your hidden soul will become a repentant heart. Then God will remove even the poverty from your heart and when poverty no longer exists, God will remain.

You see, we are at the heart of every mystic. Sanai also says, in *The Walled Garden of Truth*, this extraordinary phrase: "If your soul doesn't pass by the crucifixion on Friday, it will never make it to the resurrection on Sunday."
Isn't this the pure doctrine not only of the Sufi masters, but also of Christian mystics?

- **This brings us to asking what it is to be a Sufi.**

There's no lack of definitions.
There is this one, rather famous, of Abu Hussain al-Nouri:[6]

The Sufi is the one who has nothing in his possession and is not possessed by anything himself.

There is the definition from Abu Sa'id Abu'l-Khayr[7] who was asked what Sufism consisted of: "What you have in your mind, abandon it; what you have in your hand, give it away; what happens to you, don't try to avoid it."
There is this definition from an anonymous master: "He who is purified by love is pure and he who is absorbed by the Beloved and has renounced all the rest is a Sufi."

- **In fact, isn't the Sufi the one who is totally empty of him – or herself – to leave room for God? He or she then is entirely inhabited by the Divine.**

That's it.

- **Teresa of Avila and John of the Cross said nothing different.**

Of course. But we shouldn't forget what Rumi repeats often: "In reality, God is the seeker."

---

6. Abu Hussein al-Nouri (840–908). A prominent early Sufi living in Baghdad (a major center of Islamic culture), and author (in Persian) of mystical poetry, *Stations of the Heart(s)*. A contemporary of Hallaj, Junayd of Baghdad, and Shibli. His friends and followers called him Nuri, meaning "radiant" in Arabic.
7. Abu Sa'id Abu'l-Khayr (December 7, 967 - January 12, 1049). A famous Persian Sufi and poet who contributed extensively to the evolution of Sufi tradition.

In the last analysis, as I have already written, everything is based on love. God, as is mentioned in the Qur'an, is closer to human beings than they are to their own jugular vein. If they know how to love, mystics discover the Divine within their own hearts. God declared through the voice of the Prophet: "The earth and the heavens cannot contain me, but I am contained in the heart of my faithful servant."

In fact, to return to the definition of a Sufi, I can, as I said, give you many, but I prefer to say, as did Rumi, that it is indefinable.

Rumi marvelously illustrated this by the parable of the elephant[8] which you probably know, but that I cannot resist the pleasure of citing:

> The elephant was in a dark house; some Indians
>   had brought it to exhibit it.
> In order to see it, several persons entered the darkness,
>   one by one.
> The first one reached the trunk.
>   He said, "This creature is like a water hose."
> The hand of the next one touched the ear:
>   it seemed to him like a fan.
> Another, having grabbed the leg, declared,
>   "I find that the form of the elephant is like that of a pillar."
> Another touched its back and said,
>   "In truth, this elephant is like a throne."
> In the same way, each time someone heard the description
>   of the elephant, he understood according
>   to the part that his hand had touched.
> According to the place that was "seen," their observations differed.
>   One man called it the letter "l" and the other the number "1."
> If they had all taken along a candle, the differences would
>   have disappeared from their perceptions.

This example also means that you can only express what you feel yourself and there are as many paths as there are pilgrims.

- **In other words, there are as many definitions of Sufism as there are Sufis.**

You have understood exactly!

---

8. The parable of the elephant was originally from the Indian subcontinent, cited in Jain, Hindu, and Buddhist texts. Sanai records it in his *Walled Garden of Truth* as a teaching story known to Rumi.

- **Under these conditions, you can at least look for what are the common points for all the Sufis and even of all the mystics.**

I would like to reply with two quotations taken from Rumi's letters:

> And if any one puts his trust in God, He is sufficient is for him [her, them] (Qur'an 65:3).[9]

And [from Rumi],

> I will not be satisfied with a drop of water
> You have to throw me into your river.

- **What the Christians called abandonment or surrender to Divine Providence?**

Yes, to which you must add praise, which is its natural consequence.

It is so very important to be grateful and give praise. Listen to what Rumi said on this subject:

> When God on high wishes to bestow his grace, his favor, his generosity, and his felicity in a long-lasting manner to one of his servants, He accords them the happiness of giving thanks. If a hundred bitter subjects come to them, and one sweet one, they celebrate this sweet one a hundred times, in a hundred places, while they do not even repeat once the hundred bitter subjects, with the exception of the bitterness produced by separation from the companions of faith.

- **All this leads us more and more to the heart of Sufism which is, we believe, the constant search for Unity.**

Rumi wrote: "Our *Mathnawi* is the boutique of Unity and whatever you see there besides the Unique is an idol."

I could cite you, just from the works of Rumi, hundreds of texts on Unity, on the fusion of the Sufi with the Divine. It's really a matter of a relentless nostalgia that pushes the lover of God to try to find that lost Unity, more than anything else. Outside this Unity, we are living an illusion.

---

9. The ongoing mention of both genders, "men and women," throughout the Qur'an text was remarkable for its era. The aim for inclusion is clear.

- **I think I'm hearing a Buddhist lama.**

And why not? They also know this nostalgia and your lama could applaud with both hands on hearing this text of Rumi:

> When man and woman become one, you are the One;
> When unities are erased, you are this Unity,
> You fashioned this "I" and this "We" in order to play
>   the game of adoration with Yourself,
> In order that all the "I's" and "you's" become one single soul
> And, in the end, be immersed in the Beloved. (*Mathnawi*)

Or yet another, also taken from *Mathnawi*, these admirable verses:

> If you drink water from a bowl when thirsty
> It is God that you contemplate within the water.
> Those who are not lovers of God see in the water their own image.

We are all like the famous pillar (tree stump) in the mosque in Medina. The Prophet used to preach leaning against it. One day, a chair was placed in the mosque. On seeing this, the pillar began to sob. The Prophet held it in his arms and asked it what it wanted so much, and the pillar replied, "My heart is torn by the separation from you."

- **That's so beautiful! We would like to ask you for even more citations and stories. I think we could listen to you for days on end.**

It's true, you certainly don't get bored with Rumi. To respond to your request, here are two texts that illustrate perfectly what that Unity he desires with all his heart represents for him.

The first is taken from Rumi's text, *Fihi Ma Fihi:*[10]

> In the presence of God, two "Is" cannot exist. You say "I" and the Divine says "I." Well, either you die before God or God dies in front of you, so that duality would cease. But it is impossible and inconceivable that God should die, because God is by definition, the Living, the Immortal. . ..
> So because it isn't possible that God dies, your self has to die to allow the Divine Self to reveal Itself to you so duality can disappear.

---

10. Translated into French by Eva as *Le Livre du Dedans*.

V

• **And the second text?**

It's taken from *Mathnawi*:

> A lover asks her lover: "Who do you love more: you or me?"
> He replies: "I am dead to myself and living through you;
> I have become non-existent concerning myself and my
> attributes and exist through you; I forgot my own aware-
> ness and know only through your awareness; I lost every
> idea of my own power and have become powerful through
> your power."

We could go on for a very long time.

• **Is it you, of course, who translated these texts?**

Yes. All the texts that I cited are already in my books, but I am
happy to share them with you.

• **Rachel and I often recite to each other this verse of
the *Diwan*: I am your lute, it is you who play each of
my strings and make them resonate.**

I already spoke of the role that music and dance played for Rumi.
He compares himself constantly to a musical instrument played by
the Beloved.

> We are the harp and it is You who play our strings.
> We are the flute and our music comes from You.

The dance itself, the *sama*, we have already mentioned, for the dervish is nothing but a means to merge with his God. He dances like
the atoms of creation.

• **I must admit that we didn't believe our ears when
you spoke of his knowledge of atoms.**

It's certainly surprising. Rumi is the man of blazing intuitions.
Everything he said, for example, about evolution is striking.

• **Surely you don't mean to imply he's a precursor of Darwin?**

Of course he doesn't express himself the same way, but he nonetheless has a very clear vision of the chain of evolution that goes
from mineral to vegetable, from vegetable to animal, and from
animal to human. To my knowledge, no one before him said such

striking things on this subject. I must admit I was stupefied to discover this text for the first time:

> From the moment you came to the world of existence,
> A ladder was placed before you to allow you to escape.
> First, you were mineral, then you became plant;
> Later you became animal, how could you ignore it?
> Then you were made human, gifted with knowledge, reason
> and faith;
> Consider this body, drawn from the dust: what perfection it
> acquired!
> When you will have transcended the condition of being
> human, you will no doubt become an angel;
> Then, you will have finished with the earth: your home will
> be in the sky.
> Go beyond even the angelic condition: enter this ocean,
> Allow your drop of water to become a sea.

- **In a way, he goes well beyond the evolutionary point of view. He doesn't stop with the human being. The purpose of evolution for him, if we understand correctly, is to arrive at a point where we lose ourselves in the Infinite. Can we believe something like this? How can we become conscious that such a marvelous thing is waiting for us at the end of our road?**

He anticipated your objection or, if you prefer, your disbelief. He imagined an embryo inside its mother to whom one would describe the external world and its marvels. Of course, the embryo could not possibly believe it. This poem is certainly one of Rumi's most surprising and most beautiful works.

> If someone said to the embryo inside its mother:
> "Outside of here is a world very well arranged,
> A land so agreeable, long and wide, filled with pleasures
> and things to eat,
> Mountains, seas, plains, fragrant orchards, gardens
> and sown fields,
> An exalted sky, full of light, the sun, rays from the moon
> and a hundred stars;
> The south wind, the north wind, the west wind, giving gardens
> the appearance of banquets for weddings and feasts.

These marvels are beyond any descriptions:
    why do you remain miserable in this obscurity?"
The embryo, because of its present state, would be incredulous,
    would reject this message and not believe it.
Saying, "This is absurd, this is trickery and an illusion."
    For the judgment of the blind is devoid of imagination.
Given that the embryo had not perceived anything of this sort,
    it cannot listen (to the truth).
Just as, in this world, the saint talks to ordinary people of the
    other world, saying, "This world is a dark and narrow
    grave, beyond is a world without odor or color."
None of their words can enter the ear of any of them,
    because sensual desire constitutes an enormous, solid barrier.
Desire shuts the ear and prevents it from hearing;
    the attachment to self closes the eye and prevents it from
    contemplating.
Just as in the case of the embryo, the desire for blood,
    which is its nourishment in its vile residence,
Prevents it from lending an ear to news of the world.

Rumi speaks constantly of the joy of the afterlife. For him it is the natural culmination of life and we have been created just so that we may one day know it. He is constantly enthralled by it and his meditations sometimes lead him down strange paths. For example, when he evokes the drop of sperm that has neither hearing nor intelligence, and yet from it is born the human body, so complex and harmonious. He watches the development of organs and the rise of intelligence. This incredible evolution cannot *not* have a purpose, and this purpose, he affirms constantly, is to arrive at heaven, whose "very nature is to expand the soul with joy."

This is how he sees his mission: To awaken people, to make them realize that their destiny goes well beyond this earth, that they are called to awareness and to a radiant future they cannot begin to imagine.

There's no time to lose, and the spiritual guide is there to motivate people to get moving without delay.

"If we let ourselves become drowsy," he said in evoking his mission, "who can take care of those unfortunate ones who sleep? I have taken all of them as my responsibility, to ask God to bring them to perfection."

For Rumi, the human being is meant to be whole [complete, perfect]. Without a doubt this is the basic intuition of Rumi: Knowing that human beings can always improve and that the role of the spiritual guide, in the last analysis, consists of letting individuals become what they are capable of being. The guide is a midwife who must bring into the world this complete human being that we are all called to become.

- **I understand now why you told us one day that he was the perfect spiritual guide.**

He was, and he still is. To use one of his images, he sees himself as the servant who wants to stir the milk in the churn so the hidden self, inside each person, can be liberated like the butter, just like the taste of butter that liberates itself from the milk.

VI

- **Death must have been an apotheosis, a culmination for Rumi.**

It was indeed. All over Turkey, the anniversary of his death is called "the wedding night." A few days before his death, Rumi asked someone who had come to wish him good health:

> "When I am going to unite with eternity, the night of my wedding, why do you want me to stay here?"

He also said to Sheikh Sadruddin, who came to his bedside,

> "When between the Lover and the Beloved there is nothing more than a linen shirt, don't you want light to be united with light?"

He died on December 17, 1273, at sunset. In Konya, every year on this day, there is a great dance of the dervishes which, in recent times, has unfortunately become a little too touristy.

- **His funeral must have been grandiose.**

Magnificent! We know a lot about it, because it was described by Aflaki [biographer and hagiographer of Rumi and his disciples]. All the local inhabitants were there, the Muslims, but also the Christians and Jews, because everyone identified with him. Everyone was crying, moaning, and tearing their clothes. Anyone who knows crowds in the East would have no difficulty imagining that day. The Jews were part of the funeral procession, reciting Psalms, the Christians, the New Testament, and no one would have dreamed of stopping them.

There had never been such universal ecumenical spirit. The sultan was astounded by it and called in the leaders of the Christians and the Jews to ask for an explanation. Why were they celebrating a Muslim?

Aflaki records their answer: "In seeing him, we understood the real nature of Jesus, of Moses, and of all the prophets; we found in him the same perfect conduct as our prophets as we read about them in our books. Did not Rumi say, "We are like a flute that, in one mode, harmonizes with two hundred religions."

- **For us who, thanks to you, have been able to read Rumi, this is the main point, the absolute tolerance born of the certainty that there is only one Divine Spirit loving one and all, and that the profound experience they have of this relationship is similar for seekers of all faiths.**

That's exactly why I was drawn to Rumi when I was allowed to discover him.

- **To the point of dedicating your life to him . . .**

Of course. What could possibly be more important? When I am in Konya, I often think of the funeral of Rumi, of the crowd, of the call to prayer, of the funeral chants . . .

And from among his poems, I like to recall this one that he wrote at the end of his life:

Our death is our wedding with eternity.
What is its secret? God is one.
The sun is divided in passing through the openings of the house;
When the openings are closed, the multiplicity disappears;
This multiplicity exists in the clusters of grapes
It does not exist in the juice that comes from the grape.
For the one who is alive in the light of God
Death of this carnal soul is a blessing.
On this subject, say neither good nor bad
Because it has gone beyond good and bad.

- **I imagine that the place where he is buried is even today a place of pilgrimage.**

Of course, and even more, it's the heart of Konya. From a distance, you see the dome of his mausoleum with its enamel tiles reflecting the sun. It's a veritable place of peace with its trees and fountains that never stop singing.

Inside, the tomb appears immense. It is placed on a platform surrounded by a silver balustrade and is draped with a sumptuous cover embroidered with verses of the Qur'an in gold letters. The faithful do not kiss the tomb directly, but rather the two steps that lead to it. The light is very soft, from lamps hanging from the ceiling.

Rumi is not alone in the mausoleum. He has near him his son, Sultan Valad, who continued his work, as well as Rumi's father Bahauddin Valad, who, according to the tradition, wanted to die standing, out of respect for the Prophet who came to the edge of Paradise to welcome him. There is also a collection of treasures, including rich illuminated manuscripts of the Qur'an and the *Mathnawi*, carpets of Anatolia, musical instruments, clothing that belonged to Shams and Rumi, as well as a carpet given to him for his marriage.

In the courtyard are cells, because there was a monastery there until 1925, the date at which Mustafa Kemal Atatürk abolished the Sufi orders. You can still see the refectory and the vast hall where, every Friday after prayers, the dervishes did the cosmic dance. All this has become a museum, but it remains very moving.

- **Can everyone go inside, even the "infidels"?**

Of course. I have always admired in Rumi this universalism, not always shared by everyone. Over the entrance of his mausoleum is inscribed this warm, inclusive invitation: "Come, come, whoever you are, here is the dwelling place of hope."

In addition, I am persuaded that it is no coincidence that he moved to Konya in his youth and remained there all his life.

- **You wrote a whole book about Konya.**

Yes, because it's not an ordinary city. It was the first city to be evangelized. You seem surprised. Perhaps you don't realize that Konya is the Iconium of St. Paul.

Recall that after his enlightenment on the road to Damascus, he was received by Ananias,[1] who hid him in his house, a house that I visited in Damascus, on Straight Street.[2] Ananias helped him to escape because things started to go badly for him. Paul fled with Barnabas, who was originally from Iconium. So naturally they headed for this city. So this is why I said to you that it was the first city to be evangelized. Later, it was also here that Timothy began his missionary career.

---

1. Ananias of Damascus. 1st century disciple sent to heal Paul after he was blinded on the road to that city, and then to baptize him (Acts 9:17-19).
2. Roman Via Recta, currently called Zoqaq Mustaqim, both meaning Straight Street, beginning at Damascus's Eastern Gate (Bab Sharqi), cited in Acts 9:11.

Legend has it that Paul preached in the house of a certain Onesiphorus. Just in front of this house lived a beautiful young girl named Thecla. According to *The Travels of Paul and Thecla*, an apocryphal story popular in the first half of the 2nd century, the mother and the fiancé of Thecla denounced Paul to the governor of Iconium. The young girl was said to have given all her jewelry to obtain the liberation of Paul, who had become her spiritual father. Condemned to be burned at the stake in the main square, she was miraculously saved and later left to follow Paul.

You can still see today, near the city, the Church of St. Thecla, which must be one of the oldest churches in the world.

Allow me a brief digression: few people know that the epistles of Paul were written between twenty to twenty-five years after the first writing of the Gospels. And do you know how we were able to date them? It's a very curious story: In the Epistle to the Romans, Paul said, "The eleventh year of the fourth triumphal campaign of Claudius, I went to see the brothers in Jerusalem. . . ." Unfortunately, we didn't know when the fourth triumphal campaign of Claudius occurred.

About twenty-five years ago, a British archaeologist wrote to a scholarly organization in London that he had just found in Cyprus a votive marker from the fourth triumphal campaign of Claudius. This marker, after technical calculations, allowed us to date the Epistle to the Romans as Easter of the year 56, that is, twenty-four years after the first version of the Gospel according to St. Mark.

You see, Konya is thus a very important city for the Christians. They rediscovered it later thanks to Jean de Plan de Carpine,[3] the ambassador of Pope Innocent IV to the Mongol court. He traveled there on the way to his mission with the great Khan of the Mongols in Karakorum.[4] He described it as "beautiful Iconium," a city as beautiful as Cologne with a multitude of bell towers.

A little later, it became the Konya of Rumi, and, as a result, during two centuries, Konya experienced a period of absolutely

---

3. Giovanni da Pian del Carpine (ca. 1185-1252). Italian Franciscan monk, archbishop, explorer, and historian. Also known as Jean de Plan de Carpine, he was sent by the Pope, then based in Avignon, France, to the Central Asian court of the Mongols and met with the ruling Khan Güyük during his visit. He subsequently wrote *Ystoria Mongolorum (History of the Mongols, Whom We Call the Tartars).*
4. The physically challenging journey, including time at the Mongol court, took place between 1245 and 1247.

extraordinary religious synergy. It was not just tolerance – I don't like this word because it always evokes a certain condescension. It was really an embracing universalism, which, let me point out, is the essential nature of true Islam.

That this nature is not generally what is being practiced in today's world has nothing to do with the essence of things.

- **We can certainly ask ourselves why this universalism has been replaced by intolerance.**

It happened gradually. You know, colonialism didn't help much. When there is violence on one side, there is always a response to it.

- **But this universalism seems to have stopped well before colonialism.**

Not from the point of view of thinking. There was perhaps a sort of sclerosis or ankylosis.[5] Of course, colonialism didn't begin with the conquest of Algeria or Indochina. Already on May 18, 1190, the Crusaders took Konya by siege, but were unable to take over the palace of the sultan. And later, once the Crusades were over, there were all those missionaries who tried to convert the Muslims, thinking they were doing good, when in reality they did much harm.

- **Nor were the Muslims beyond the same actions. Do you believe they didn't try to convert the Christians?**

No doubt. And as time passed, things became even more harsh. Unfortunately, that's what often happens! Christianity of the early days became harsher and harsher, council after council, in order to combat heresies.

- **Islam probably did the same thing.**

If you will, but this was less spectacular because the word *heresy* doesn't even exist in Islam. One speaks rather of "unfortunate innovations,"[6] which is a little more elegant.

Rumi himself was completely free of the least contamination of intolerance. You can still feel it today if you spend some time in Konya. He loved his city a great deal and his son tells us that he blessed it often in these terms:

---

5. Hardening or stiffening.
6. Arabic, *bid'ah*, undesirable innovation, straying from the path.

From now on, give Konya the name "City of the Saints" because every child that comes into existence here will be a saint. So long as the blessed body of [Rumi's father] Bahauddin Valad and those of his descendants are in this city, it will be sheltered from the sword; its enemies will not achieve their goals and, finally, will perish. It will be ensured against sorrows till the end of time. If even a part of it is ruined and destroyed and if its importance declines, nonetheless it will not be demolished totally; because even if it were ruined, our treasure will remain buried there.

• **That reminds us of St. Francis's blessing of Assisi.**

But you know, I could cite numerous episodes of the life of Rumi that irresistibly evoke the *Fioretti*.[7]

• **Just tell us a few of these stories. They will go straight to our hearts because we love St. Francis.**

They say that one day St. Francis silenced the birds that were preventing the audience from hearing his sermon. Well, Rumi did the same thing with the frogs. One day he had assembled his disciples near a pond and the frogs made such a racket that he shouted at them with a loud voice, "What is this uproar? Is it your turn to speak or ours?" The frogs stopped immediately and were silent until the moment when Rumi signaled them to continue their concert.

Like St. Francis, he lived in total harmony with nature. "The trees," he said, "recognize me and respond to my greeting." Like St. Francis, he had a burning love for all creatures. One day when he was troubled by the look of a steer being taken to the slaughterhouse, he purchased the animal to save its life.

Another day, a disciple was astounded to hear Rumi ask him to go and buy a lot of fancy meat pastries. This was not a habitual request because the Master was, as you can imagine, extremely austere. The disciple went to buy the delicacies and gave them to Rumi who, without saying a word, took them, covered them with

---

7. *The Little Flowers of St. Francis* in Italian, *Fioretti de San Francesco*. Collection of stories about the life of St. Francis compiled more than a century and a half after his death. The text is inspired by the saint's work and is drawn in part from his writings. The document itself is now attributed to Ugolino Brunforte (c.1262-c.1348).

a napkin, and took off. Intrigued, the disciple couldn't help following him. "I walked very quietly behind him," he later said, "He went to some ruins where I saw that a dog had had puppies. The Master gave all the provisions to feed the dog. I was stupefied by this compassion, this pity. 'For seven days,' he told me, 'she has had nothing to eat, because, due to the little ones, she couldn't leave them. God transmitted her cries to my ears and commanded me to help her.'"

Isn't that just like a typical Franciscan story?

Of the cities I know, three resemble each other in the atmosphere of gentleness and faith that envelops them. You've probably guessed them: Konya, Medina, and Assisi.

You know, the spirit of great saints permeates the cities they inhabited. Centuries and centuries after their death, you can still feel their presence and if you pay attention, you can sense the thirst for the Absolute that they experienced throughout their lives.

This thirst that Rumi describes:

Get up, O lover,
Show some impatience:
The sound of water,
You're thirsty
and (yet) you sleep!

Inside, the tomb of Rumi appears immense. It is placed on a platform surrounded by a silver balustrade and is draped with a sumptuous cover embroidered with verses of the Qur'an in gold letters. The faithful do not kiss the tomb directly, but rather the two steps that lead to it. The light is very soft, from lamps hanging from the ceiling

VII

- It's strange. The first time we met with Muslims to write *Prophets of Today*, we were full of fear and concerns. We still had in our ears the dire predictions of Khomeini, and now you, who became a Muslim, are talking to us about universalism and love.

I'm talking to you about Rumi and the Sufi masters of yesterday and today who are beings of tenderness and openness. I should say that in reading them, in translating them, I went from one sense of wonder to another. I could cite you examples by the hundreds of their universalism.

To stay with Rumi, one day he wrote in the *Discourses of Rumi* (*Fihi Ma Fihi*) that the paths that lead to Mecca are certainly diverse. One can go by land or by sea, by Byzantium or by Syria, crossing large or short distances. But what difference do the paths make? Isn't the point to arrive in that place where, suddenly, the discussions and controversies cease, in that place where hearts open and unite? "This uplifting of the heart," he says, "is neither faith nor infidelity, but love."

He welcomed everyone who came to him without even asking them what religion they belonged to. He even had a very close friendship with the Bishop of Konya. After the death of his first wife, who had left him two young children, he married a Christian woman who had recently converted to Islam.

Throughout the ages, this tradition of universalism within the order did not weaken. In the 17th century, one of its members, Assur Didi, even became a famous specialist on the Torah and the Gospels. Indeed, the order has always been marked by the absence of fanaticism, drawing toward it disciples from other confessions whose beliefs were respected.

I don't want to over quote, but this paragraph, drawn from a letter from Rumi, seems to me to illustrate perfectly what I just said:

So, as the prophets recognize each other, if you don't admit one of them, it's as if you don't admit any of them. In fact, it is one light that appears through different windows and that reaches you through the person of each prophet. If you refuse one part of this light, that shows that you are like a bat that says, "I am opposed to the sun from this year, but I accept the sun from last year." In fact, the sun from last year and from this year are not two, but the same one. But the difference is that you didn't experience what the sun was like last year.

- **What you say touches me very specially. When I was little, the priests in my high school constantly said that you had to believe, and that filled me with confusion and discomfort because, in fact, believing is not all that easy. You can't force yourself to believe. In any case you can't really believe externally because they tell you to believe. That was a path that seemed impossible to me, as if I already sensed that belief – faith, if you [109] prefer must come from inside, from a Presence that is in us.**

Exactly. I am perhaps too intellectual, but I am not capable of knowing what God is like. I cannot visualize God and I don't want to. But I know that there is an Absolute, beyond all that one can know or imagine. When you see that a spermatozoon can become a Mozart or an Einstein, you cannot *not* think that there is a form of intelligence behind all this. There is an Absolute, but one that may or may not reveal itself.

If the Absolute doesn't reveal itself, you have a religion like Buddhism in which, through successive purifications, you climb the steps of a ladder at the end of which you begin to have a small idea. When Buddha replied to his disciples who asked him about the immortality of the soul, he answered like the father whose little six-year-old son wanted to ask about Einstein's Theory of Relativity: "We will talk again after you've studied physics." In essence, the Buddha replied to his disciples, just like a father, "We will talk again when you have attained a sufficient level of consciousness."

Inversely, the three Abrahamic religions agree that the Divine does reveal itself to humanity. This revelation teaches us that God is merciful, but [nonetheless] cannot be revealed in a fundamen-

88

tally different manner to the Chinese, Indians, or Arabs. God is necessarily the same for all. The fundamental message is the same, that Divine Spirit is the Essential. All the rest is merely a reflection of something revealed that you can interpret different ways.

- **Do you mean that in the Essential, beyond the interpretations, everything comes together?**

Of course.

- **But do you find this sense of universalism in the Qur'an?**

Let me give you just two quotations.

The Qur'an says [as part of verse 2:262] that . . . if you are Christians, Jews, or Sabeans (author's interjection: the Sabeans were famous idol worshipers at the time), and if you do good, you have nothing to fear from your Lord.

The Qur'an also says that . . . if God had so willed, he would have made you one single religious community, but instead, he wanted to enlighten you using your differences. So, do good, support one another and God will enlighten you in time concerning your differences.

- **So we constantly return to what is fundamental.**

Exactly. What is fundamental is to say from the bottom of your heart and your thought that there can be no divinity other that the Supreme Reality. That is something all believers of all the traditions can affirm. As Simone Weil said, polytheism is not about believing in Jupiter or other gods, but to worship money, or power, or authority, or a way of thinking.

There can only be this Truth, this Reality. The rest is just tales people invent. All right, we don't drink wine, we fast for Ramadan or for Lent, and it's good that we do. I don't drink wine because it doesn't seem necessary to me *not* to conform to a recommendation of my community. Drinking or not drinking alcohol is not the main point [of religion].

One day, in Algeria, I believe I shocked certain Muslims when I said, "I believe that it is worse, forgive me for being judgmental, to make a cutting remark about someone than to not fast during Ramadan."

• **But rituals are necessary.**

Yes, but the ritual should mainly serve to cement the community. It is especially necessary to Islam which, without it, would run the risk of becoming a sort of metaphysical deism, a sort of *Weltanschauung*,[1] a vision of the world that is very universal, very ecumenical, but a little vague. Ritual was necessary to form the community: the five prayers per day, Ramadan, et cetera.

What I find truly remarkable in Islam is that prayer is cosmic. It is linked to the seasons, to the moon, to the sun. It's communion with the sacred cosmos. The *Fatiha*, the equivalent for us of the Lord's Prayer, is a completely cosmic prayer, because you pray standing like a tree, kneeling like a human being, and prostrated like a rock. You take in your hands all of creation to offer it in the name of humanity. It's the part of the prayer that we always say in the standing position, the only one that we say in the plural. It is the first prayer said in the ear of the newborn and the last that you murmur to the dying. It accompanies all the serious circumstances of life. And when you complete it, you turn your head to the right and left and call for peace for the world.

A Bedouin in his desert knows when the prayer time is by looking at the length of shadows. The date of Ramadan is set by the moon. I would say that prayer in Islam is set to the resonance of the sacred cosmos.

This is not always easy, because there is no possibility of anthropomorphism. It is easier to contemplate the face of Christ than to be alone before the Absolute.

• **But there's the Prophet Muhammad.**

But you never pray to him. You're not supposed to pray to him.[2]

• **We have heard a lot of stories of people who dream of the Prophet Muhammad. They told us that when he came to them in a dream it was a blessing.**

Yes, but no more than when you dream of St. Francis of Assisi. As

---

1. Literally, world view.
2. Muslims, based on a Qur'an verse (33:56), do ask the Divine to bless the Prophet. "God and His Angels send blessings on the Prophet: O ye who believe! Send your blessings on him and salute him with all respect." (Yusuf Ali translation). The Qur'an also enjoins believers on multiple occasions not to distinguish among the prophets.

I already mentioned, for a true Muslim, the Divine is worshipped, not saints.

- **There are still people who visit the tombs of holy men (*marabouts*).**

There are, but it's a practice that is not recognized by the religious authorities. People obviously need consolation and to have something closer to them, but the cult of saints is frowned upon. It's a little like praying to St. Anthony of Padua[3] to find something lost.

Besides, these cults can't become fixed or institutionalized because there is no supreme earthly authority in Islam, no pope or councils.

This allows for great latitude regarding what you should or shouldn't believe.

- **Could you give us an example?**

Take the case of reincarnation, of successive lives.

- **Don't tell me that Muslims are free to believe in it or not.**

Of course they are! You know that the founding fathers of the Church often believed in it, including Origen.[4] Then there was a decree made by the Church in 585, I believe, at the Council of Mâcon, which declared that people who believed in reincarnation deserved excommunication.

Islam, because it doesn't have councils, cannot forbid belief in reincarnation. There are certain ideas that may be said to be not very orthodox, but there can be no notion of heresy because there is no one to describe that which is heretical or not. If someone claimed, for example, that a person could be reincarnated in an animal body, I suppose that in a reasonably conventional Islam, he would be considered a little out of line. It doesn't seem possible that, after arriving at the human level, a soul could be reincarnated in the body of a duck or an ant. People might say that he was

---

3. Saint Anthony of Padua (1195-1231). Born and educated in Portugal, later joined the Franciscan order and was widely respected for his stirring sermons and efforts to help the poor and the sick. Also known as the patron saint of lost things.

4. Origen Adamantius (about 185-245 C.E.). Egyptian scholar, philosopher, and prominent early Christian father in Alexandria. Some of his writings point to reincarnation, others do not.

a little crazy, but if he insisted, he would not be excommunicated.

- **There have, nonetheless, been martyrs in Islam for heresy.**

Yes, but very few. You may say that that's still too many. You're thinking, no doubt, of al-Hallaj. You must understand that for a very long time he was in open conflict with his prime minister and, because he was enthralled with God, literally, drunk with God, he walked around the streets of Baghdad proclaiming, "I am God, I am God." I think that in any even slightly orthodox religion, this would not have been tolerated.

- **It was for the same reason that Jesus was crucified.**

Yes. Rumi wrote some beautiful pages about this:

> We consider that it is the ultimate pride although in fact it is the ultimate humility, because al-Hallaj meant "I am nothing. Only God exists." The man who declares "I am the servant of God" claims that two exist: himself and God. But the one who says "I am God" has disappeared. Saying "I am God" is to say "I don't exist. God is everything, nothing exists except God."

Al-Hallaj could have escaped punishment by denying what he had said, but he refused. What is strange is that his best friend Shibli,[5] who was also a great theologian, attended the trial without protesting the verdict. When he was criticized for this, he declared, "I feel very sorry for him, but why did he foolishly reveal the inner secret of the heart?"

I also believe that some of his friends didn't interfere because such an attitude ran the risk of becoming clearly sacrilegious. Others could have proclaimed themselves God without having experienced, like al-Hallaj, transformational union.

Try to understand, I don't want to say that the Muslims are white as snow, and I am the first to realize that, especially nowadays, you can't say that. But in the final analysis, based on facts, you can count on the fingers of one hand the Muslims who were tortured because of their faith. I don't need to remind you regarding torture, that there were dozens, if not hundreds of thousands

---

5. Shibli (861-946). Sufi mystic and scholar, disciple, and successor to the celebrated Sufi master, Junayd of Baghdad.

in the Christian world. No one was burned at the stake in Islam.

- **There is an extraordinary and startling parallelism between the crucifixion of al-Hallaj and Jesus.**

That's true, and with respect to Jesus, I'd like to quote you something from Ibn Arabi:[6] "I believe that Jesus is God, but I do not believe that God is Jesus." He meant by this that Jesus became God because he eliminated himself to such an extent that he was totally filled with God. This is the transformational union that I spoke about earlier.

Let me add, but I believe I already mentioned that the mystics in Islam compare the book of the Qur'an to the human person of Jesus. Both are means of transmitting the message: Christ in his physical person and by his words, and the Qur'an in writing. You also realize that you cannot be a Muslim if you do not recognize the Torah and the Gospels as sacred books.

- **We have strayed a bit from reincarnation but we haven't exhausted the subject yet. Can you say that there are Muslims today who believe in reincarnation?**

Of course there are! Many Sufis believe in reincarnation, but purely individually.

- **Maybe the Sufis do . . .**

But the Sufis are Muslims.

- **Yes, but . . .**

You can't be a Sufi without being a Muslim, but you can be a Muslim without being a Sufi. It's very important to emphasize this point because very often, with a little bit of spiritual racism, the people who consider Muslims horrible will immediately add, "Oh, the Sufis, well, that's different! We consider them out of the mainstream." That's like saying that Teresa of Avila was a Roman Catholic but not a Christian. Sufism is not at all out of the mainstream. In the context of Islam, Sufism is an experience of internalizing the living faith, obviously including great freedom of thought, which

---

6. Ibn Arabi (1165-1240). Prominent Arab scholar, philosopher, and Sufi mystic. Sometimes referred to as the greatest sheikh (Sheikh al-Akbar), his philosophy included the notion of Unity of Being or (*Wahdatul-Wujud* in Arabic), which presents the case that all that exists is one being.

is also characteristic of essential Islam.

If there is one rule, it is that everyone should understand the Qur'an as if it had just been revealed to him or her at that very moment.

• Could you give us an example?

The Qur'an says,[7] ". . . from one stage to another people are transformed, but they do not understand because they are forgetful.[8]

Does this mean a purely spiritual evolution in the context of a single life? Does it mean the Greek *lethe*, the forgetfulness between two incarnations? You can understand it as you wish.

• Again, do you personally know any Muslims who believe in reincarnation?

Indeed, I do, and not insignificant ones. I already mentioned that because there is no ecclesiastical hierarchy in Islam, there is no supreme authority, but there are still some people who are considered more advanced than others. For example, the late former rector of the prestigious University of al-Azhar, in Cairo. He was the one who invited me to Egypt and he became a very good friend, just as he was also good friends with the Indian politician Krishna Menon.[9] Well, he told me that he fervently believed in reincarna-

---

7. The expression "As the Qur'an says . . ." is quite useful and used in discussions related to the Qur'an so that a conversation can go on normally without stopping a speaker who does not necessarily recall the precise words of the verse itself. This practice, used between students and scholars at al-Azhar University in Cairo and in other locations, allows the merits of the comment to be examined, and naturally the Qur'an text itself, in Arabic, remains the standard for the verses themselves.

8. This verse was cited by the author as part of a long interview in French, now translated into English. The original Arabic is from Qur'an 56:60–62: "We have decreed Death to be your common lot, and We are not to be frustrated from changing your Forms and creating you (again) in (forms) that ye know not. And ye certainly know already the first form of creation: why then do ye not celebrate His praises?" (Yusuf Ali translation). The Qur'an itself acknowledges on multiple occasions that people are transformed over time, as well as reminding them that they do not always reflect clearly or understand correctly. In addition, it points out that humans are inclined to forgetfulness.

9. V.K. Krishna Menon (1897-1974). Indian nationalist and politician, militant supporter of Indian independence, High Commissioner to the UK after independence, later head of the Indian delegation to the United Nations. Menon was a close friend and supporter of Jawaharlal Nehru (1889-1964), first prime minister of India after Gandhi's assassination.

tion and he found it in the Qur'an.

You've no doubt heard of Amadou Hampaté-Ba, who was the Malian ambassador to UNESCO. At the same time, he was the Grand Sheikh of one of the largest Sufi orders of sub-Saharan Africa. I met him after he was already in poor health, and I remember that one day I went to see him in the hospital. I asked him, in a roundabout way, what he thought of successive lives. "Of course, we believe in them," he replied, "We even teach about it in our orders, but to a very select group. We would not want to encourage less mature disciples to say that with all eternity ahead of them, they can make all the imaginable and possible mistakes in this lifetime. We only discuss the matter with a very limited number of advanced disciples."

Note that in India, it is often said, "If this poor man died of hunger, it is because he was very bad in a previous life." It is to avoid this type of reasoning that the Sufi masters remain discrete on the subject.

- **Now we understand why you are so comfortable in Islam: If you can interpret the Qur'an as if it had just been revealed to you that moment, you have the same liberty of conscience so dear to your Protestant grandmother.**

You're right: I found the same freedom.

Given the verse previously mentioned, "From one stage to another people are transformed, but they do not understand because they are forgetful." Amadou Hampaté-Ba saw the *lethe*, the forgetfulness, between incarnations, while another could say, "Not at all! This means that people have a spiritual evolution within the course of a single life, but they always forget." Neither of the two would be a heretic.

- **When we hear you, we always have the impression we're hearing the same kinds of things Sheikh Bentounes would say. We met him for our book *Prophets of Today*, and we were struck by his radiance as well as by his sense of universalism. Do you know him?**

Of course, and for many years. I'm delighted you have given me the opportunity to speak about him because I have a long-standing friendship with him and his Sufi order, filled with much respect, admiration, and deference. I find him extremely open. He had no idea that he would one day be the head of this order, and he experienced some frightening moments before accepting the position. All the people I have sent to him have been struck by his light and by his radiant goodness.

One of his disciples told me that someone had said to him, "I am a Catholic and, since I met the sheikh, I am a much better Catholic than before." When the sheikh heard that, he exclaimed, "Oh, how wonderful!" That's just like him. The order of the sheikh to which I am attached in Morocco is very linked to the order of Sheikh Bentounes and, if I need advice on spiritual direction, I may ask Sheikh Bentounes rather than my own sheikh because he is far away and doesn't speak French at all.

- **Sheikh Bentounes must be very sad, like all the other Sufis, to see the rise of fundamentalism in Algeria. What are the relationships between the Sufis and the extremist movements?**

Sufis have always resisted the fundamentalists. Indeed, they were often persecuted by the moralists, like mystics in other religions. Wasn't St. John of the Cross held in prison?

- **When we first met Sheikh Bentounes, we were expecting to meet an elderly gentleman with a beard in a flowing robe. We met a young man, completely modern.**

He is perfectly luminous, serene, and at the same time, he has embraced his era. His Sufi order helped computerize the Qur'an, so children can study both religion and computers at the same time. He has a lot of insight. I introduced him to several of my friends who wanted to become Muslims and, each time, he insisted that they not rush. "Be sure about what you do," he repeated constantly, "and only make a fully conscious commitment."

Sometimes, when I happen to be feeling down, which fortunately doesn't happen often, I catch myself saying to myself, "If Sheikh Bentounes were in Paris, I'd take a cab and go see him."

- **What struck us is how many Westerners are members of his order, especially young people.**

That's true and I'm very happy about it. It is marvelous that there are still people like Sheikh Bentounes. I see him as the antidote to fundamentalists.

- **In fact, he reminds us constantly that all that really matters is Presence.**

You remind me of these words of Rumi:

> Whatever we say is merely vain talk in comparison with vision; all these words merely substitute for vision; they are not for the one who is present, but for the one who is absent.

I, who have talked so much with you recently, would like to insist that we must be suspicious about words. They bring about errors and contradictions.

Do you remember the parable of the four people of different nationalities who all wanted grapes, but couldn't agree on what they wanted because each called them different names? They quarreled endlessly although they all wanted the same thing.

The mystic is above all a seer of the invisible. He or she lives for this purpose. One day they asked Bayazid how old he was, and he replied, "Four years old." They said, "How can that be true?" and he responded, "For seventy years this world hid God from me, but I have seen God during the last four years. The period during which one is veiled cannot be counted as life." (This photograph was taken a few feet from Rumi's tomb.)

VIII

- I'd like to play the devil's advocate. I agree with you one hundred percent about everything you've said during the past two days and am very happy to hear what I hear, but still, I'm forced to note that this doesn't correspond at all, really not at *all*, with the idea we have here about Islam. No doubt that's because we are talking about the ideal Islam of the Sufis.

Of Rumi, of Iqbal, of Sheikh Bentounes . . . The list is long.

- This is the Islam that we love, open toward the universal. It's very well and good, but it's certainly not the Islam of the holy war, of the famous jihad.

Indeed not.

- So, what do we see in the Islam of today, as well as throughout history? An intolerant religion, violent, with forced conversions. A constraining religion, puritan to the extreme, which reduces women to slavery. At least that's the idea that the majority of people have here [in France, in Europe]. Are they completely wrong? In other words, I would like you to reply in advance to all that these people will say, especially to those who will accuse you and us of bad faith, of being naive, of living on a pink cloud.

This is very important. Let me return to Iqbal, whose ancestors were Brahmins and who was born in the Punjab to Muslim parents. He started to study philosophy in India, then in Germany and England. His studies were so brilliant that some of his teachers themselves translated some of his works. That's how Nicholson translated his *Mysteries of the Self*. Iqbal did not intend to bring a personal message. He only wanted to expose the concept a modern Muslim could have of Islam. He wrote:

Islam does not teach the renunciation of this world but condemns the attachment to materialism. It considers that human beings can aspire to well-being in this life and to well-being in the afterlife.

In *Gabriel's Wing,* written at the end of his life, Iqbal tries to show that self-awareness and action are the two essential poles. He wanted his philosophy to have an application at the human scale and with a universal scope.

- **Excuse me, but you're not responding to the question we asked you. They will accuse you of describing an ideal Islam and not the Islam that is real and practical.**

You're right, but can't we say the same thing about all religions? Certainly, the Islam we see outside is not often at the level of its principles, but isn't the same thing true of Christianity? Wasn't its task to transmit a message of love and universal peace? So, we can talk about Christianity according to its principles, about the Christianity of mystics and authentic saints, but we can also talk about intolerance, the massacre of the Cathars, of St. Bartholomew's massacre, and the fundamentalists of today.

Because we are not making a sociological study, we should base our discussion on principles. And the principles of Islam, like those of Christianity, appeal to love, tenderness, and universalism.

- **Could you give us some examples?**

If you like, let's talk about the role of women in Islam.

- **A favorite weapon for those who criticize Islam.**

Precisely. To be fair, we must put principles on one side and sociological reality on the other.

I was struck, for example, by the liberty of women in Pakistan. I recently met two young Malian women returning from the pilgrimage and I made the mistake of saying, a little hypocritically, "When your parents choose a husband for you . . ." They jumped all over me and said, "When we bring our parents a young man who pleases us to ask for their agreement, well, that will be more like it." They could talk and live this way because the society of Mali is not the same as that of Saudi Arabia.

In Cairo, the Indonesian women students were freer than the

women students from Libya, Sudan, or even Algeria. It appears [to Westerners] that the sociology of North Africa, in general, is not particularly feminist. But do you believe that it is very different from the sociology of Sicily or of Sardinia? Is the Italian "mama" with her numerous children and her black scarf so different from the North African "mama"?

I believe that you should compare comparable things, comparable social classes, and comparable cultural settings. A professor of law in Cairo is as different from a villager in Algeria as a law professor in Milan is different from a villager in the middle of Sicily. Besides, if we go too far into sociological comparisons, we'll never reach an understanding.

To me, it's not that Islam is blocked or behind the times. It is the functioning of Islamic societies which has not kept up. To cite a concrete case, there are many possibilities given to women in Muslim law that they can take advantage of and put in their marriage contracts. It also is true that they frequently don't do so.

- **Could you give us an example?**

For example, even if the wife is confined in an insane asylum, their husbands do not have the right to take a second wife.[1] It's written in black and white. The unfortunate thing is that in less developed circles, people don't know the law and the possibilities it offers. The Grand Sheikh of al-Azhar said to me one day, "I would like you to teach our daughters to be more aware of their rights. They would certainly by much happier."

Unfortunately, they suffer from the weight of customs, superstitions, and traditions that are just as constraining in far-off villages in Greece, in the south of Italy, and in Spain. It's just the Mediterranean world that is like that.

What you have to see is what is in the texts.

---

1. It would appear that the author has misspoken here. The original text, based on six hours of interviews made in two consecutive days, said the husband could not remarry, which in fact he may, but he is not legally allowed to evade his family responsibilities.

- You can't deny that, in an era when people are talking every which way about a "renewal" of Islam, whether it's in Iran, in Algeria, or perhaps tomorrow in Morocco, not to mention Saudi Arabia, in [many] people's minds this "renewal" is associated with even more intolerance, violence, fundamentalism, and enslavement of women.

Unfortunately, I cannot, but I must repeat, because many do not want to hear it, that it's a sociological problem. You are looking at facts that are religious in appearance, but in fact have nothing to do with the essence of religion.

- But how can this have happened? You said that Islam has the advantage of not having a hierarchy, but it certainly seems that the hierarchy is behind this neo-fundamentalism.

There is no hierarchy, but there are some narrow-minded opinion makers who disapprove of postcolonial society, with blanket judgments devoid of nuance. The people [often victims of European colonialism] imagine Western women as promiscuous. It would be difficult for them to imagine a nice middle-class French family with a grown daughter who looked like a loose woman.

It's a shame, but what do they see in the West? Pornographic films, risqué literature, miniskirts, bare breasts on the beach . . ..
None of this is very serious, but it shocks something basic inside them.

The political leaders take advantage of this, but the Islam they claim is an Islam of protest, not Islam itself.

It's disturbing, I agree, but it's the result of some ambitious or so-called enlightened people who cause a lot to be said about them, though they are far from having the importance you are giving them. I have Algerian, Moroccan, and Egyptian friends who are perfectly feminist in the good sense of the term. For them, feminism does not consist of being nude on a beach, but of being able to wear a bathing suit like everybody else.

I would like to go further to the heart of the matter: The biggest problem in Islam today is that Quranic law is, as it were, included in the Qur'an. That makes reform difficult.

It seems to me the Roman Catholic Church experiences the

same type of difficulties. The law on remarriage of divorced people [before more recent reforms] seems terribly harsh and unfair to me. I knew the daughter of a French aristocrat who lost her parents when she was very young. She was brought up by a grandmother whose only fear was to die before her granddaughter was "taken care of." Well, she married her off to a man who seemed very nice but who abandoned her without a word to go to America. They never heard from him again. This poor girl found herself, from one day to the next, without money, without a profession, and with four children to take care of. If there had been a nice guy who wanted to be a good husband and a good father to her children, she would have had to choose between him and her religious life. This is unimaginable and cruel.

• **What would happen in a comparable case in Islam?**

You can remarry.

• **Is divorce allowed?**

Of course. Divorce can be requested by each of the partners, without either of them having a sense of transgression.[2]

Let me be clear. Leave sociological problems aside and return to the texts. In all the principles, the woman is not considered as an inferior. When the Qur'an speaks of fundamental rights, it refers to "Believers, men and women," "Muslim men and women." A woman has the same rights over her husband as the husband has over his wife.

• **Not with respect to inheritance.**

That's true. The inheritance of a sister is half of that for a brother. I remember in the beginning that horrified me until I understood why it was this way. Note that you cannot take a legal prescription out of context and examine it in midair, as it were. You need to realize that in Islamic law, marriage is always under the rule of separate property. If the husband goes bankrupt, the wife does not have to pay. If she works, if she inherits or receives gifts, she can do what she wants with them. In one way, she is even more indepen-

---

2. "If a wife fears animosity or desertion on her husband's part, there is no blame on them if they arrange an amicable settlement between themselves; and such settlement is best; even though souls are prone to avarice. But if you are virtuous and reverent, truly God is aware all that you do" (Qur'an 4:128).

dent than the man, because he is required to maintain his wife, his sister, or his near relatives.

Take an example: The parents die and leave a daughter and a son. The daughter receives only half of what her brother gets. But she can use her share as she wishes. She is responsible for nothing. Her brother, on the contrary, must support her. He is also supposed to help other members of the family who are in need, so it's not altogether unfair that he has twice the share of his sister.

- **What you say is perhaps valid for a traditional society, but even Muslims live less and less in traditional societies. Families separate in their countries as in ours, and young men are probably less supportive of their families than they used to be. In these conditions, is this law fair according to its principles but unfair according to the facts?**

A few years ago, when I represented France in a seminar on Islamic thought, I raised this question to three eminent legal scholars: the son of Iqbal, who is president of the Court of Appeals of Lahore; Ben Djelloun, who was the head of the Moroccan Bar Association; and a very famous Egyptian lawyer.

I said to them, "All this is lovely. It's fine in a traditional society, but let's take a working hypothesis: The two parents die in a car accident. The daughter stays alone in Cairo or Algiers. She has a brother who left the family at age fifteen and became rich because he moved to Chicago where he married a millionairess. He hasn't been in contact with the family for years. Are you going to send him a double share of the inheritance and let the girl starve to death in Algiers or Cairo?"

All three agreed that it would be an injustice, and that a verse of the Qur'an could not cause an injustice. From a practical perspective, because they couldn't modify a verse of the Qur'an, they would feel obliged to send the brother twice the share of the sister, but they would only send it if it were accompanied by a clause requiring that the brother only receive the money on condition that he pay the sister a monthly living allowance.

That's fair and it conforms perfectly with the spirit of the Qur'an.

Muslim law is a fascinating law because, like English law, the legal experts have broad liberty of interpretation. There is, of course, a risk that the judge be narrow-minded, but nothing is perfect.

- **Tell us a bit about testimony. The word of a man, apparently, is worth more than the word of a woman, because the Qur'an says [regarding competence as a witness] ". . . and if you can't find two men, choose a man and two women."[3]**

That's true and it really irritated me. I also asked this question to my three legal experts, who didn't have to compare notes to agree. It was perhaps justified in the past, in pre-Islamic times, when women were kept at home. But it's a rule which has become obsolete by itself.

You know, I'm a woman and I don't like macho men, but macho men are not limited to Islamic countries. There are a lot of battered wives in France, in Ireland, in the United States.

- **Still, if you can't change a line of the Qur'an, how can Muslim law change and adapt itself to its era?**

Al-Ghazali,[4] who is a bit like the St. Thomas Aquinas[5] of Islam, makes the following distinction:

There are three sorts of verses in the Qur'an[6]:

[1] Those that concern religion from a metaphysical perspective: There's only one God who is love, compassion, etc. Those verses should not be changed.

[2] Those that establish ritual. In principle, these

---

3. "And get two witnesses of your own men, and if there are not two men, then a man and two women, such as ye choose for witnesses, so that if one of them errs, the other can remind her. . ." (Qur'an 2:282. Yusuf Ali translation). This important verse about financial agreements over time is almost 20 lines long, establishing principles that emphasize the need for written documentation and witnesses to ensure fairness to all parties.

4. Al-Ghazali (1058-1111). The renowned medieval scholar, philosopher, and mystic of Persian origin, who wrote his major works in Arabic. He is credited with encouraging understanding between Islamic orthodoxy and the Sufi tradition. He was considered a renovator of the faith during his lifetime and given the honorific title of "Proof of Islam" for his masterwork "The Revival of Islamic Sciences.

5. Thomas Aquinas (1225-1274). Italian Dominican friar, jurist, theologian, who synthesized the philosophical works of Aristotle with the principles of Christian scripture. One of the giants of Roman Catholic theology and philosophy.

6. These categories are quoted by the author from the writings of al-Ghazali.

should not be changed, but there could be exceptions. For example, the fast is not an obligation for pregnant women, sick people and travelers.

[3] Those that concern personal relationships, from personal status to commercial dealings, etc.

Al-Ghazali, who died in 1111, said on this subject, "It's obvious that the last category should change with the era." This is precisely the work of thinkers and jurists whose reason for existence is, to use the title of Iqbal's book, the reconstruction of religious thinking in Islam.

- **Give us an example of what can be reviewed.**

Usury is forbidden in Islam. In the Middle Ages, the usurer was seen as a greedy, mean master who lent money to his serfs during bad seasons and later squeezed them until they gave up.

But in our day, can we talk about usury when you establish, for example, an aviation company with shares, bonds, and interest? Certainly not. The funds can and should be compensated. This is not usury because there is a counterpart of risk taking that didn't exist before.

All the Muslim jurists that I have met are at least in agreement on this point. Islamic law must take into consideration the evolution of the times.

- **And polygamy? Last year we met Moroccan women who explained to us the following: The Prophet, living in a time when polygamy was a respected institution, couldn't abolish it. No more than Jesus, in his time, could give women the place that he obviously would give them today. The Prophet did everything he could to regulate this custom. Later, Muslim men acted in opposition to the profound thinking of the Prophet.**

I agree, and I knew you would ask me this question. Here, too, we need to refer to the text and to the era when it was captured in writing.

What most people who say just about anything about polygamy don't realize is that it is extremely restricted. Before the time of the Prophet Mohammad, women in Arabia were merely objects, and polygamy was practiced without any limits. The Prophet could not abolish it overnight and he probably didn't even think of that, but he limited it considerably.

You need to realize that in the beginning of Islam, there were large numbers of men killed in war. Mecca was a commercial center where prostitution flourished and where orphans and widows had no means of earning their living. They either died of hunger or became prostitutes. It was better to be someone's second wife. That is what the following, often-cited verse implies:

> If ye fear that ye shall not be able to deal justly with the orphans, marry women of your choice, two, three or four: but if ye fear that ye shall not be able to deal justly (with them), marry then only one . . . (Qur'an 4:3).

What does this mean exactly? This means that polygamy was an exceptional measure for exceptional cases but that the rule was monogamy, and the above verse clearly states you must be fair.[7]

As the Qur'an says in that verse, "Marry only one, it is better for you."

Of course, later, men, chauvinist as they can be, didn't take account of the true spirit of the Qur'an.

Furthermore, you should note that Islamic countries don't all have the same attitudes concerning polygamy. In Turkey, for example, a country with separation of church and state, polygamy is strictly banned. Turkish women voted and piloted planes before French women could. They have extreme liberties. I'm not saying this is always true out in the countryside, but that's a matter of sociology.

Tunisia, as well, does not allow polygamy.[8]

Pakistan has an intermediate position that seems to me to conform to Muslim law. A man who wants to marry a second wife must address a court and give his reasons. If he says "I've been married for twenty-five years, but I fell in love with my secretary and I

---

7. The Qur'an affirms that humans cannot be fair in such matters: "Ye are never able to be fair and just as between women, even if it is your ardent desire: But turn not away (from a woman) altogether, so as to leave her (as it were) suspended. If ye come to a friendly understanding, and practice self-restraint, Allah is Oft-forgiving, Most Merciful. If the two separate, God will enrich both out of His Abundance and God is All-Encompassing, wise" (Qur'an 4:129-30, Yusuf Ali translation).

8. Tunisia became the first Arab state to ban polygamy in 1956 and Tunisian women, regardless of their religion, are now free to marry non-Muslims.

want to marry her," he would not [likely] be given permission. But he can obtain permission if he has a wife who is an invalid or who is confined to an asylum.

In general, to summarize, we can say that polygamy is never a good thing and should only be admissible in very special cases.

- **If you had a Muslim husband, would you accept that he bring a second wife to the house?**

Oh no, I would rather divorce him. You know the Prophet Muhammad was more liberal than you realize. They say that one day, a young woman came to see him, and they had the following dialogue:

> Woman: "I want a divorce."
> Prophet Mohammad: "Your husband isn't kind with you?"
> Woman: "Yes, he's very kind."
> Prophet Mohammad: "He doesn't give you whatever you need?"
> Woman: "Yes, he spoils me."
> Prophet Mohammad: "So, what isn't working?"
> Woman: "I don't love him. My parents married me off and I never agreed to it."
> Prophet Mohammad: "If that's the case, you are free."

This attitude became unimaginable later, but this little story implies that it was men who subsequently harshened the teaching to take advantage of it.

- **Tell us about the holy war, this famous *jihad* that frightens so many people in the West.**

It's a contradiction in terms. *Jihad* means "struggle," and Islam [as clarified by the Prophet Mohammed himself] considers that this struggle is waged against our sins and against ourselves [our egos]. It's really an internal struggle.

Coming back from an expedition, the Prophet said to his companions[9] one day:

> "We are returning from the minor war. Now, we must turn ourselves to the major war against sin."

Now *that* is the real *jihad*.

---

9. The people who followed the Prophet Mohammad at the time were called his companions.

Politics makes the so-called holy war that you are speaking about. Religions, unfortunately, are not led by saints. Often politicians are calling the shots and use religion for their own purposes. When they want to conquer territory or increase their power, they say that it's a holy war. But the idea of a crusade is in no way limited to Muslims.

- **Put yourself in the place of the average person who sees what's happening in Tehran.[10] Today, many people have the impression that there is a Muslim peril.**

You shouldn't overlook Western colonialism, nor that there is a reaction to it. The Algerians [in the 19th and 20th centuries] didn't come to France, but rather the French invaded North Africa and later Indochina. After all, it was the Europeans who massacred the Aztecs, the Mayans, and the Incas and destroyed these great civilizations. And what have we done in Africa? All this is relatively recent. The abolition of serfdom in Russia only goes back to the last century. I find that in the West we are quick to give ourselves a clear conscience.

I don't like the fundamentalists and I detest what was done in Iran [during the time of Khomeini], but you need to realize that it's a reaction. I went to Iran during the time of the Shah. It was not very nice.

- **After him, it didn't get better.**

No, and that's what we call being between the horns of a dilemma. Even among those who detested the Shah, many today are sorry that he is no longer there. At the same time, the secret police were abominable. During that time, I found Iran completely unpleasant. There was a sort of exaggerated westernization that eventually brought about a reaction of rejection. I remember ordering a salad one day in a restaurant. They served it with bacon. I said that I didn't eat pork and they told me that's the way it is served. Another time, I was invited to the Grand Hotel in Shiraz. The menu only included hamburgers and things like that. Everything was enveloped in loud rock music, difficult to tolerate. At 4 a.m. American businessmen returned to the hotel drunk and slammed their doors. It was an imitation of, a caricature of America. In Shiraz, I

---

10. The text was referring to the time of Khomeini's rule in Iran in the 1980s.

had hoped, after all, to have some good Persian cuisine with some nice traditional music.

Of course, Khomeini and his excesses were abominable, but they exemplified rejection.

- **To the point of imposing the chador [the head-to-foot veil]?**

Let's talk about the chador! That is not at all Islamic. The Qur'an requires women to be dressed decently, but it never says for them to wear a veil on their faces. When I went to Mecca for the pilgrimage, I saw Yemeni women arrive with veils on their faces. They made them take them off. Poor things! They looked as unhappy as I would have been if they had asked me to take off my blouse.

You must be careful not to confuse a veil over the face and a scarf.

There's a charming story related to this that shows that during the time of the Prophet, women were not veiled. At the end of his life, he was walking with a young companion when a young girl stopped him and said, "Oh Messenger of God! My father is very old and would like to make the pilgrimage. Can I make it in his place?" The Prophet gave her permission and turned to his companion, who was about seventeen or eighteen and said, "Do you think this is really the moment to be looking at the face of a pretty girl?"

You know, [some] journalists write just anything. Take the case of lapidation [stoning]. One day, Henri Fesquet[11] asked me to write an article for the newspaper Le Monde about the stoning of women who had committed adultery in Iran. I consulted all the competent experts, and they all agreed that lapidation was certainly not Islamic.

It is already difficult, if not impossible, to prove that adultery has taken place. I'm sorry if I shock your chaste ears, but the Sheikh of al-Azhar, who is a very fine man, very straitlaced, reminded me

---

11. Henri Fesquet (1916-2011). French journalist who returned from prison camp in Poland after World War II, and was invited to join the staff of the then new newspaper, Le Monde, founded by Roman Catholics. A practicing Catholic, he had respect for and great interest in, other religions. He wrote a column on religion in general, and readers appreciated it. Intellectually curious, he was open minded and humble, with a sense of fairness. In a country not known for being particularly interested in religious matters, his column appealed to a diverse audience and flourished.

one day that to prove adultery, you need to have four witnesses, with the condition that they not be family members or friends of the accusing spouse.

Take a typical case: A husband leaves on a trip and says he won't be back for a few days. He returns the same evening and finds his wife in the arms of another man. What can he do? He can hit the man, but that's about it. If he wants to divorce claiming adultery, he must furnish four witnesses, eye witnesses who *saw* the act itself. The Sheikh of al-Azhar pointed out to me, "You should not be able to pass a thread between the two bodies." You see it's not simple.

Even if it were simple, the punishment has never been stoning. The Qur'an says, "Even if they have committed adultery, if they repent, forgive them."[12] If you stone an adulterous woman to death, you prevent yourself from being able to pardon her and thus you are no longer faithful to the intention of the Qur'an. I finished my article for *Le Monde* by telling this story: The Prophet received a woman in Medina who was overcome with remorse and said to him, "Oh Prophet, I have committed adultery." She repeated the statement three times and he finally told her, "Drop it and move on." I put this text in parallel with the phrase of Jesus who said with respect to the adulterous woman, "Let him who is free from sin cast the first stone."

I'm not saying that stoning has never occurred at the hands of enraged people claiming to be Muslims, but I affirm that it is abominable and has nothing to do with Islam.

But it seems we are talking too much about sociology because, I repeat, all these questions of veils, inheritance, polygamy, and stoning are sociological problems that have nothing to do with the basis of Islam, the Islam of mystics and saints to which I have devoted my life.

Among these mystics and saints, there have been many women who often had many disciples: the daughter of Sultan Valad, for example, and another woman from Konya, 'Arifa Hosklika, and then the most famous of all, Rabi'a.

She enchanted me particularly because she was full of love and humor. Attar spoke a lot about her in the *Memorial of Saints*. She

---

12. "If two men (or two women) among you are guilty of lewdness, punish them both. If they repent and amend, leave them alone; for Allah is Oft-returning, Most Merciful" (Qur'an 4:16, Yusuf Ali translation).

was also a woman of common sense, as indicated by the response she made to a man who came to her to confess his numerous sins. "If I repent," he asked her, "will God turn toward me [one of the Arabic expressions for forgive]?" "No," she replied to him, "but if God turns toward you, you will repent."

She lived during the 9th century and is the first great woman Sufi in Islam. She was formerly a singer and not a courtesan as people have often said, but rather more like a geisha. She was a slave, but her master freed her after listening to her pray. She wrote very beautiful poems, some of which have been translated by Massignon.

She often reminds me of Teresa of Avila.[13] Do you remember this story? One day Teresa was traveling to see one of her convents in one of those horrible carriages of her day. She crossed a river, fell into the water and said to the Lord, "If this is the way you treat your friends, I understand why you have so few of them." One day Rabi'a expressed the same sentiment. She was in her little room and decided to fast all day. She had left a bowl of water, a candle, a glass of oil, and a piece of bread on a shelf. Her evening meal was to be the bread dipped in oil with the water to quench her thirst and the candle allowing her to read the Qur'an before sleeping. At the end of the day, right when she was waiting with a certain impatience for the moment to eat and drink, a cat jumped on the shelf and spilled the water, which put out the candle and soaked the bread. With nothing left, she, like Teresa, let herself grumble to her Lord. Then she heard a voice asking her, "Which do you prefer, my love or your meal?" Of course, you can imagine, she quickly responded, "Your love, Lord."

I love the familiarity of these two women with the Divine. Rabi'a was very well known in her day. Famous men, great Sufis, were not embarrassed to go and consult her. Joinville[14] speaks of her, several centuries later, saying that she ran through the streets holding a bucket of water in one hand and a torch in the other. The water, she said, was to put out the flames of Hell and the torch was to burn down Paradise.

---

13. Teresa of Avila (1515-1582). Carmelite nun, Roman Catholic Saint, Spanish mystic, widely published and read author, even today. Named Doctor of the Church in 1970 by Pope Paul VI.

14. Jean de Joinville (1224–1317). Renowned chronicler of medieval France. He authored *The Life of St. Louis* including the chronicle of the Seventh Crusade.

She wanted so much for her prayer to be unselfish that she constantly repeated, "Oh Lord! If I adore you out of fear of Hell, burn me in Hell. If I adore you in the hope of Paradise, keep me out of Paradise. But if I adore you for you alone, do not hide your eternal beauty from me." She was truly the first songster of pure love.

- **We again return to the Essential.**

Yes. Like all the mystics, Rabi'a wanted to go to a total renouncement, to the void, to that passiveness of spirit that Rumi illustrated one day by this parable comparing the approach toward the God taken by theological students and Sufi mystics:

> One day, he says, a king called to his palace painters from China on the one hand, and from Byzantium on the other. Naturally, both the Chinese and Greeks claimed to be the best. The king challenged them to decorate two facing walls with frescos. A curtain was drawn between the two groups of competitors, who each were painting a wall without realizing what their rivals were doing. But while the Chinese employed all sorts of paint and made a great effort, the Greeks merely polished their wall and unrelentingly smoothed its surface. When the curtain was opened, you could admire the magnificent frescos of the Chinese painting reflected in the opposite wall, which shone like a mirror. All that the king admired in the wall of the Chinese seemed much more beautiful on the facing wall.

And Rumi goes on to explain:

> "The Greeks are the Sufis. They are without studies, without books, without erudition.
> But they polished their hearts and purified them from desire, from covetousness, from greed, and from hatred."[15]

It is always, in the final analysis, a matter of the external dialogue between the philosopher and the mystic, between those who talk about God and those who experience God, a dialogue that will never end and will always result in a stalemate. Logical reasoning is often compared to the cane of the blind. Only an open ear can seize the essential of the Essential and understand in its profun-

---

15. This story was taken by Rumi from al-Ghazali's *The Marvels of the Heart*.

dity this marvelous couplet from Rumi:

> What God said to the rose, and which made it bloom in beauty,
> God said to my heart and made it a hundred times more beautiful.

The mystic is above all a seer of the invisible. He or she lives for this purpose.

One day they asked Bayazid[16] how old he was, and he replied, "Four years old." They said, "How can that be true?" and he responded, "For seventy years this world hid God from me, but I have seen God during the last four years. The period during which one is veiled cannot be counted as life."

- **It seems here we are rejoining the New Testament and the famous discussion with Nicodemus: Jesus replied, "Very truly I tell you, no one can see the kingdom of God unless they are born again" (John 3:3, New International Version).**

That's right, and that's why the fully realized human being, the ultimate goal of all seekers, is defined by the Sufis as one who is born again and is completely aware of his or her essential unity with the Divine Being in whose image she or he is made.

This is what Rumi calls the spiritual resurrection, recognizing this essential resemblance to the ultimate Reality, after transcending the illusion of duality.

- **Excuse me for citing you, but you wrote in *Mysticism and Poetry in Islam*:**

The perfected or complete human being is the reason for the existence of the cosmos, because he or she is the intermediate link between the Divine and created things. Because God wanted "the treasure of divine love and generosity to be revealed," God uses the holy person as a means through which to reveal the Divine Self to creation. The double role of the realized person flows from this.

That's exactly right. To know oneself, as Rumi says, is to discover

---

16. Bayazid Bastami (804-874). Persian Sufi from central Iran. Known as Sultan al-Arifin (King of the Gnostics). Renowned for publicly expressing the mystic's complete absorption into the Godhead, he was one of the pioneers of what later came to be known as the "ecstatic" (*sukr* or *sakran*) school of Islamic mysticism.

God in oneself. That reminds me of the famous parable of the poor man in Baghdad.

He spent all his inheritance and was in abject poverty. After he addressed ardent prayers to God, he dreamed that he heard a voice telling him that there was a treasure hidden in a certain place in the city of Cairo. He left and, arriving in Cairo without any money, he resolved to beg, but he was embarrassed to do so before nightfall. Because he was wandering in the streets, he was seized by a squad of police who took him for a thief and beat him up before he could explain himself. He finally managed to tell about his dream with such a tone of sincerity that he convinced the police lieutenant. The latter said, "I see that you are not a thief, that you are a brave man, but how could you be so stupid as to make such a long voyage based on a dream? I have often dreamed of a treasure hidden in Baghdad in a certain street in the house of someone and it never caused me to travel there." The house that he mentioned was the house of the traveler. The latter then praised God because the cause of his misfortune was his own fault, and then he returned to Baghdad where he found the treasure buried under his own house.

It's a beautiful story, and like all Sufi stories, it goes much farther than it appears. Why go looking so far away, when the One we seek with all our might is hidden within our own heart?

- **The more we listen to you talk, the more we are under a spell. You have learned so much and you have so much to teach. After all, do you think that the fact that you're a woman kept you from being received as you should have been?**

It's not a problem at all. The more the people that you meet are advanced on the spiritual path, the easier it is.

Something extremely rare happened to me. One day when I was at Cairo University, I received a telephone call from a sheikh I didn't know and who asked me, "Are you free next Friday? I need you at the mosque in Heliopolis." Heliopolis is an elegant suburb of Cairo, a little like Neuilly, near Paris. There is a large mosque there where I was supposed to go after the Friday prayer.

I arrived on time at the door and asked the guardian where the door for women was. "It's over here," he said, "but, madam, they're expecting you at the entrance for men." I put my shoes back on and went back to the other side and found an assembly of about two hundred men who were seated on the floor. The prayer had just ended. There, seated near a small table, was an old sheikh with a gray beard I didn't recognize. "Ah, Doctor," he said, "Come sit beside me." I asked him what for and he replied that I would see. I sat down feeling awkward, without understanding what he wanted from me. Then he took the floor: "I have asked you to come here because I want all these men, some of whom are hostile to girls' education, to know that, while being a mother and a Westerner and a university professor, you can arrive at Islam through studies. Will you please tell us about the path that brought you here?"

I said that my Arabic wasn't good enough, but he asked me to speak in English and said he would translate. I told about my journey and when I stepped down from the dais, all these men wanted to shake my hand. It was extraordinary. I was sure that some of these men, in the course of that presentation, had prejudices dissolve they had held since their childhood.

These prejudices are not always as entrenched as we might think. A few years ago, I visited the old part of the city in Algiers with the conservator of historic monuments of Algeria. He wanted to show me how, during the war, you could go from balcony to balcony to escape from the French special forces. In fact, he had a son who died under torture by them, but he was without bitterness because he had been able to forgive.

At a certain moment he said, "It's time for the prayer, but if we all try to go to the main mosque, it will be over when we arrive. There's a little prayer room, but it's normally reserved for men. I don't want to leave you outside." In front of the door, there was a man making the call to prayer. My guide explained the situation and the man replied, "Of course, let her join us!" It was a little room with whitewashed walls. I stood discretely in the back, but they made a place for me. At the end of the prayer, as is often the case, they formed a circle. I took advantage of the situation to thank these men very much for having altered their custom for me. Then an old worker said to me teasingly, "Ah, madam, you distracted us so much from our prayers. We were so happy. We were saying to each other, how on earth? Here's a woman, a French woman, who is praying with us just like that. We were so happy, that's all we could think of."

IX

- **The other day while preparing for our meeting, I read a poem of Rumi that really struck me. Allow me to read it before asking my question:**

We have all been part of Adam,
　　we have heard the melodies of Paradise.

Although the water and clay (of our bodies) covered us
　　with doubt, something of these melodies
　　returns to our mind.

But mixed as they are with this earth of affliction,
　　how can these sounds, high or low,
　　give us the same joy?

This is why the sama is the nourishment of the lovers
　　of God, because it contains the image of peace.

- **In this poem, Rumi seems to say that we were aware of Paradise and that, once we came to earth, we constantly feel nostalgia for that state.**

Not only Rumi, because this is one of the essential themes of Muslim poetry and mysticism. Iqbal presented this issue very well.

It is often said that the Sufi is the child of the moment. I might add in passing that this inevitably leads to a certain aesthetic.[1]

---

1. This is in reference to the Sufi term Ibn Waqt: "The saint hath no fear, because fear is the expectation either of some future calamity or the eventual loss of some object of desire; whereas the saint is the 'son of his time' [resides in the eternal present/presence]; he has no future from which he should fear anything, and, as he hath no fear, so he has no hope, since hope is the expectation either of gaining an object of desire, or being relieved from a misfortune, and this belongs to the future; nor does he grieve, because grief arises from the rigor of time, and how should he feel grief, he who dwells in the radiance of satisfaction and the garden of concord." Al-Junayd, 9th century.

• **Could you give an example?**

Let's take a poem about autumn. If it were a Japanese poem, there would be four lines and the poem might say:

> It is raining
> The sky is gray
> My heart is sad
> The frogs are croaking.

If it were a romantic poem, it might be:

> The long heaving sobs of the violins of autumn . . .

There is a beginning and an end, while in a poem from an Islamic culture there would be a juxtaposition of couplets that each has a complete meaning by itself. These sayings are juxtaposed and interchangeable on a thread called the *hal*, which is really impossible to translate. The poem expresses the *spiritual state* of the moment. A poem about autumn would never be very cheerful. The theme, like the key of G, will be a certain melody, and the sayings, I repeat, will be interchangeable. It's like a necklace of pearls whose thread would be the general theme and the pearls would be the different sayings.

This insistence on the present instant inevitably leads to a certain vision of the world. What is important is the elusiveness, the surprise and fleeting nature of all that can be contained within an instant independent of time. That is why we say that the notion of quantum physics was already present with the Arabs because they had this notion of time which, in the extreme, can even be reversible if God wills. This was very well dealt with by thinkers like Iqbal, who was himself very struck by his meeting with Bergson.[2]

• **We again touch on the notion of recalling or remembering.**

Exactly. Indeed, the Qur'an is a recalling or remembering in clear language. I could multiply the quotations to prove it. From chapter to chapter the word *recall* comes back constantly, the remembering of what is eternal and can be understood instantly by the soul. This recollection takes place from time to time because, accord-

---

2. Henri Bergson (1859–1941) was one of the most famous and influential French philosophers of the late 19th century-early 20th century.

ing to Islam, God never leaves people without revelation. St. Paul said nothing different: "In different times, in different places, God speaks to patriarchs and prophets."[3]

• **The Hindus say about the same thing.**

That's normal because it is fundamental. I often say that Islam is a little like the common denominator of the great religions. Like your citation from Rumi where you correctly speak of *recalling* a previous memory of Paradise, we return to this point in sacred texts, whatever their origin. God constantly sent variations of this theme to the Prophet Muhammad to "recite, repeat, recall, renew, bring into awareness that which has been said so often and so often forgotten."

The word in Greek for the Gospels, *Pleromai,* means "to give fullness of meaning." It's a very beautiful word. Basically, as you well know, this recalling is constantly necessary because the great risk religions always run is to become legalistic, ritualistic, and rigid. We must constantly recall the Essential to populations and religious communities, as well as to individuals.

• **But we could also imagine that people as they are had awareness of the fullness of meaning before birth and that there was also a recalling in that sense.**

You sound like a very good Muslim, my friend. I'm laughing because it's an excellent question and I am grateful to you for asking me, especially because I should have realized it earlier.

I told you how much I love Plato. Well, I constantly find things in the Qur'an that belong to Plato, especially the notion of reminiscence. The internal recalling, in a way, the notion of witnessing, is so fundamental in Islam because you can only become a Muslim by testifying that there is no god but God.

Why is the individual a witness? Precisely because the individual remembers [parts of] the plenitude lived before birth.

In the Qur'an there is a mysterious verse that has naturally been the object of volumes and volumes of analysis. God questions all people yet to be born, while they are still in the loins of primordial Adam. God asks, "Am I not your Lord?" And these beings, who

---

3. "In the past God spoke to our ancestors through the prophets at many times and in various ways" (Hebrews 1:1).

119

are still in the mind of God, reply, "Truly you are!"[4]

So before being born or rather made incarnate, these souls took a pledge of allegiance to God, their Creator, and recognized God's suzerainty over them. The Muslim mystics often say for this reason, "If we feel a nostalgia for the Divine, it is because we have known the Divine before. If we love music, it is because it reminds us of something already heard. If we love beauty, it is because we have seen God [before] and God is Beauty."

There is this notion of testimony, and the best testimony that a person can give is to surrender to God. Note that this is an attitude that goes beyond the notion of any particular religious conversion. Very often Muslims say, "This Buddhist is a very good Muslim because he submits himself totally to Divine Spirit." Let me emphasize that in one sense this surrender is not actually possible, because it has *already* taken place beyond time, in what is our superior "Me," the great "Self" described by Rumi and Iqbal. Rumi always says that between the petty me of daily life and the great Self there is a distance larger that the sea. This concept is very Hindu, very Vedantic.[5]

There is a great distance between the petty me, or ego, and the great Self, but at the same time there is a possibility of fusion in a supra-conscience. In Western psychology and psychoanalysis, if you will, we speak of the unconscious, the subconscious and the conscious. It's like a house with a main floor and a basement. In the basement rats and spiders are teeming. If they aren't a problem, all goes well, but if they climb upstairs to the main floor, we have neuroses and psychoses.

Without questioning the accomplishments of psychoanalysis, in Islamic culture, you appeal to a supra-conscience called the *sirr* or secret of the individual. The secret, the divine spark within the human being, often forgets, but sometimes remembers.

There is a fascinating story of Suhrawardi,[6] a great mystic of

---

4. "When thy Lord drew forth from the Children of Adam and made them testify concerning themselves, (saying): Am I not your Lord (who cherishes and sustains you)? They said: "Yea! We do testify!" (This), lest ye should say on the Day of Judgment: "Of this we were unaware" (Qur'an 7:172).
5. *Vedantic* comes from the word *Vedanta*, literally the books after the four classical books of Hinduism (the Vedas). Vedanta is a system of metaphysics concerned with ultimate reality, including duality/non-duality, and the liberation of the soul.
6. Yahya ibn Habash Suhrawardi (1154-c. 1191), also spelled Suhrevardi or Sohrevardi. Persian philosopher who also wrote in Arabic, mystic and founder of the

Islam, illustrating very well what we've just said. It's the story of the peacock. A prince raised peacocks in a beautiful garden. They lived happily, ate well, and they had nothing to do but display their fine feathers. One day, we don't really know why, the prince takes one peacock and sews it inside a leather sack, leaving just an opening so it can eat and breathe. The peacock is initially very unhappy, but after a while, it begins to feel nice and warm in its sack. After a little while, everything is fine: it is used to its new condition.

From time to time, however, the breeze carries the scent of the flowers. It hears from afar the cries of its fellow peacocks in the marvelous garden and it is seized by a strange nostalgia that it cannot define. It begins to suffer as the individual who retains a memory of Paradise lost suffers. Fortunately, the prince soon decides that the test is too harsh. He destroys the leather sack so the peacock can go back to reveling in the garden.

It's a beautiful story that is about us and, as I already said, illustrates perfectly the great theme in Muslim mysticism of the Return. We are all like the peacock. We hear every now and then a beautiful piece of music and our hearts tremble. It's not really a memory. It's the *amnesia* of Plato, the reminiscence.

In Islam, souls exist before the body, so they remember. There is very much this notion of *lethe*, of forgetfulness. The Qur'an, as I said, frequently insists on the fact that people are forgetful, not only of God, but of what they really are. Everything tends toward a moment of awareness which, by definition, should be spontaneous. We also find that notion independent of time, the privileged moment.

- **Is this why you practice *dhikr*, to remember?**

Yes. In the Qur'an, God says, "Remember me, I will remember you."[7] So the practice of *dhikr* is a remembering. We remember by extinguishing mental chattering through repetition. Yes, that's what Hindus do with mantras, Catholics with the rosary, or the

Iranian School of Illumination. Born in what is now present-day Iran, he also traveled in Syria and Iraq. His work synthesized wisdom from Persian, Greek, and Islamic philosophy. He completed his masterpiece, *The Philosophy of Illumination,* in his early thirties. His work was considered threatening to the ruling order at the time. He died or was executed between 1191 and 1208. He was well known as the Master of Illumination and the Murdered Master.
7. Qur'an 2:152.

Orthodox with the prayer of the Russian pilgrim.[8]

- **If there were not this nostalgia deep within us, this recalling, over and over endlessly, why would we search further? We could live in the concrete world and that would be enough for us.**

There are many people who do.

- **No doubt, but I am persuaded that all human beings have within them this nostalgia. Some just project it onto other things.**

Of course.

- **Sheikh Bentounes told us that to be a Sufi is to remember God constantly.**

Exactly, and I cannot emphasize enough this notion of recalling. In a certain sense, in Islam the one sin against Spirit is thoughtlessness or not paying attention.

For example, when you make a mistake in the prayer and think about your taxes or the letter you haven't responded to, you should make an additional prayer called the prayer of forgetfulness. It's a request to be forgiven for not paying attention, for our lack of caring.

This notion of thoughtlessness, of forgetfulness, is essential. Whether you read the Old Testament, the New Testament, or the Qur'an, there is always someone tugging you on your sleeve, saying to you, "Wake up! You're sleeping! Get moving!" It's so simple. To be a believer, for a Muslim, is to believe in God, in God's angels, in God's messengers, in God's revelation, and in eternal life. That's it. All the rest is ritual.

- **In that case, I feel like a Muslim.**

In that sense, I hope we are all Muslims [in peace, in the broadest sense]. God sends us the Word.

- **Christians would talk about the Word.**

That reminds me of something amusing. A Catholic theologian

---

8. Also called the Jesus Prayer, or the Prayer of the Heart, used in the Eastern or Orthodox Church, "Lord Jesus Christ, Son of God, have mercy on me, a sinner," based on the Publican's Prayer in Luke 18:10-14, "Lord have mercy on me, a sinner."

told me that when they wanted to translate the Gospel of John into Chinese, they didn't find a word for *logos*. There was the word "vocabulary," which was not appropriate. The question stayed in suspense for a long time and finally, the Roman Commission on Ritual allowed them to translate it by the word "way."

- **Can we say, in the final analysis, that in all the traditions the goal of spiritual life is an awakening?**

Rumi said already in the 13th century, "I have only come to the earth to waken sleeping souls." This is the task of the spiritual guide: to provoke that sort of click that made the peacock remember having lived in a princely garden.

To simplify things, we could say that the spiritual capacities of people differ according to the extent to which they remember. In this regard, Rumi tells this parable:

> They brought Black slaves from conquered lands to Muslim countries. They sold them at different ages, some five, some ten, others fifteen. The ones who were very young, who lived many years with the Muslims and who grew old there, forget entirely the country where they were born. No trace [of memory] remains in them. But if they were a little older, more memories remain in them, and even more if they were older. In the very same manner, all souls were initially in the presence of God. Their nourishment and sustenance was the word of God, without letters and without sound. Later, those souls were brought to this world as children and do not remember hearing the word before. It seems alien to them. That is the description of those who are veiled and who are engulfed in bewilderment. There are some who remember a very little bit, and in them springs the longing for the other side. These are the believers. And there are also people who, when they hear the divine word, their former state reappears: the veils fall aside and they find themselves in union.

- **So the Sufi is the one who finds him or herself in union with God?**

Yes, and you may also prefer this brilliant definition by al-Hallaj: "What is Sufism? That your annihilation be such that you have nothing left to deny or confirm."

- **A definition that St. John of the Cross would not have rejected. That again proves, if it were still necessary, that at the summit, they all join each other.**

But of course! For this reason, in entering Islam, I never had the sentiment of renouncing anything at all. I can assure you I have no problem at all reciting the Lord's Prayer, which is a very universal prayer.

- **Basically, as we already said, the stumbling block for understanding between religions is the affirmation that Jesus Christ is the *only* son of God.**

That's right. If you are a Christian, you may not be Muslim in the institutional sense, but nothing stops you from being Muslim in the larger sense of surrendering to God.

- **We could talk endlessly about the Trinity, about Mary the mother of God, et cetera . . .**

Yes, but what for?

- **In any case, we could stop talking, look at one another, love each other, and see what we have in common, which is enormous.**

That's right. If we want to go into the details of problems, we run the risk of wasting time.

Take for example, the idea of atonement. It is impossible for Islam. You probably remember that Christmas carol we sang, "and appease the anger of his Father." The other day I reminded a Jesuit of that line and he told me that it really made him laugh.

Muslims have never denied that Jesus was a martyr for love. There is evidently one verse of the Qur'an which has been much discussed which says that they didn't kill him, they didn't crucify him, it merely appeared that way to them. "And they did not kill him, nor did they crucify him; but [another] was made to resemble him to them." Concerning this verse, there is an explanation that is not admitted by mystics in general, you know, an idea according to which a phantom would have been crucified in the place of Jesus. It's not very convincing.

IX

- **There must be some sort of official doctrine.**

Not really. Muslims are divided on this point. Some say that he
didn't die on the cross, and that he was taken down before he was
dead. They put forward the argument that he had not received the
final blow like the two thieves whose legs were broken. And also
when they stuck a spear in his side, blood came out, which tends
to prove that he was not dead. Others, and obviously I am rather
inclined to be among them, affirm that the man was indeed crucified, but the essential is that his message remains alive. I admit
that this is more like splitting hairs, but isn't the essential that he
was a martyr for love?

- **And a martyr for Truth also. He refused to water
  down the message to please some groups and that's
  why he was killed.**

Of course. You know Jesus and Mary are very important personali-
ties for Muslims. It's much more profound than people realize. In
Iran, when a little girl does something wrong, they say to her, "You
will hurt the Holy Virgin."

- **You are right to say we have so much in common.**

Of course, and I will never forget what the Benedictine abbot said
to me, which I mentioned earlier: "The good thing is that we are
saying the same thing." It's so true. Read the mystics and you will
see that profoundly, beyond the institutions to which they belong,
they are all living the same experience.

He returned to his original Catholicism, at the same time being very familiar with Muslim mysticism, and he lived all his life as if paying a debt to the idea of hospitality. The idea that Christ was the host of the tabernacle was very important for him. He was a man who was committed.

X

- **I notice that you have talked very little about your spiritual guides. I believe you have a sheikh in Morocco.**

That's right, but he doesn't want people to talk about him. He's a great spirit and he has many disciples. He has given me much, but I can't really say anything else.

- **Could you at least talk to us about Louis Massignon, who played a major role in your research?**

He's someone who helped me enormously, from every perspective, and a great scholar who honored me by prefacing my first translation of Iqbal. He helped me discover many things that I would have completely ignored.

- **When did you meet him?**

A little after World War II ended. After I returned from the Resistance, as I mentioned, I joined CNRS, the French National Council for Scientific Research. I was very sick for four years, with a very serious case of anemia that wouldn't let go, probably because I was starving during the whole war. During that time, I found Massignon.

He was an extraordinary man. I know that in the Muslim world people were always very astonished that knowing Islam so well he didn't convert. In fact, he was a mystic who was beyond dogma and theologies, and he was also very intellectually curious by nature. He was from Brittany, and his world was filled with signs and symbols.

My husband died of a stroke right in front of me, in a matter of seconds. He bent over, and I thought that he was playing with the children, but then he fell down. In my distress, I called Massignon first. A little later, at his home, when we were talking about my husband, I asked him, "It's all very well to believe in eternal life, but in the end, will we at least find a smile?" He replied, "My dear girl," (that's what he called me because he was exactly my father's age) "when my mother died, I asked myself exactly the same question. I was walking one day in Baghdad thinking about her when a small boy came and offered me a dove. There they call these doves 'Haqqi' because *haqq* means truth, and doves make the sound "Haqq! Haqq! Haqq!" When the small boy offered me his dove, I thought that it was the response of my mother."

I must admit that I am not attuned to such signs, but for a spirit like Massignon, it was a symbol conveying a message. Something like this was the origin of his conversion. He tells the story in *Parole Donnée [I Give My Word]*. An agnostic, he had studied Arabic with Maspero.[1] His military service took him to Iraq, where he was responsible for making topographical relief maps for the geographic survey of the army.

Around 1914, the authorities there took him for a spy and condemned him to death. He tells the story beautifully about how they put him in a sort of basement where he was waiting for them to come and take him to be shot. From the small window, he saw the reflection of a river. I don't remember whether it was the Tigris or the Euphrates. He who, as he said, didn't believe in much of anything, thought about his mother who had died recently and cried to al-Hallaj, whose biography he had already written, "Save me, al-Hallaj!" At that exact moment, he recounts, "I felt very small and trembling in the hand of God like a small desert fox in the sand." He was in that state when they knocked on the door to announce that he was free. The people he was staying with had testified in his favor and, during that troubled time, they were gravely endangered by doing so.

His entire life was changed completely from one day to the next. He remained haunted by that ideal of hospitality, epitomized by those people who had saved him at the risk of their own lives.

Evidently, when he returned to France, he went to see all the

---

1. Gaston Maspero (1846–1916). Famed French Egyptologist and linguist who also taught archaeology and the Ancient Egyptian language at the Collège de France. He headed the mission that led to establishing the French Institute of Oriental Archaeology, providing the basis for studying discovering, analyzing, and protecting Ancient Egyptian monuments from theft as well as the elements. The Egyptian National Radio-Television Office is named for him, and that neighborhood, on the bank of the Nile, is still called Maspero.

priests he knew. He wanted to become a monk, but they advised him to get married. He often said "I, who wanted to be a monk!" which, you might note, was not very nice for Madame Massignon. She was not overly formal about it. "You know, my dear," she told me one day, "My husband is a saint." She let out a sigh and added, "It's not always amusing to be married to a saint." I'd have to say that this exceptional man was almost pathologically generous: he gave away everything he had in the house.

He returned to his original Catholicism, at the same time being very familiar with Muslim mysticism, and he lived all his life as if paying a debt to the idea of hospitality. The idea that Christ was the host of the tabernacle was very important for him. He was a man who was committed. He lay down in front of the first tank leaving for Algeria. He also never valued possessions. Madame Massignon once told me that during the Algerian war, as the dedicated mother of a family, she hitchhiked to Brittany for provisions to feed her five children and her husband, while he, in her absence, gave away all the food in the house to whomever came by.

I often went to see them, and one day I was seated in the library off the living room, separated by a glass door. I heard not shouts, because they were very courteous people, but the rumblings of a dispute. Finally, Massignon opened the door and, raising his hands to the sky, called out, "Ah, my dear girl! Women, women! I am called all sorts of names by my dear wife because in her absence, I gave my best suit to a prisoner who came by and needed it so much. My wife tells me that I shouldn't have given him the best one." He appeared stupefied by her blindness. "After all, my dear girl," he added, "I really couldn't give him anything else." I asked him why this man had been sent to prison. He knew it was for political reasons, but he was incapable of telling me whether he belonged to the F.L.N.[2] or the O.A.S.[3] It is true that for him it was no big deal to give away his clothes, because he was completely indifferent to

---

2. The Front de Libération Nationale (National Liberation Front) was the principal nationalist political party during the Algerian War (1954-1962) with a mission to wage war against the French colonial presence in Algeria.
3. The Organisation Armée Secrète or O.A.S. (meaning Secret Army Organisation) was a short-lived right-wing French dissident paramilitary organization during the Algerian War. The O.A.S. carried out terrorist attacks, including bombings and assassinations, in an attempt to prevent Algeria's independence from French colonial rule.

what he wore. I always saw him with the same old raincoat.

I went to him when I wanted to become a Muslim. He also sent me to see his friend, the bishop of Strasbourg. I told Massignon about our conversation, which moved him deeply. Massignon had a keen intellect and, at the same time, he drowned his responses in a flood of other things and sometimes gave the impression of being muddled.

I was forty at the time. He always told me, "Come by whenever you like," but I didn't dare, knowing that he worked enormously hard. I looked for pretexts; I told him that I hadn't understood this or that and asked him to clarify it for me. Then he would talk to me for two hours. I told myself that what he said was very interesting but that it didn't really respond to my question. The next day, suddenly, I would realize that he had replied in an extremely pertinent way. You simply had to extract the response from all that he had said to me. People who live in a world of signs and symbols are often like that.

He lived a sort of strange form of Christianity: he was a dolorist,[4] perhaps because he discovered God through the poverty of the underprivileged. He was especially attracted to the suffering Christ. He had an extremely austere life: he wore a hair shirt and he occasionally beat himself.

- **That doesn't sound at all like you.**

Indeed not, but I didn't learn about this until after his death when reading a dissertation written about him. Everything about him was based on participation in the difficulties of others, by fasting and prayer. There's no doubt that for this reason he experienced such an attraction for al-Hallaj, who was crucified.

- **Do you think al-Hallaj practiced self-mortification?**

I don't have any idea. Perhaps to fight with certain tendencies, to arrive at a certain purification, a certain detachment he did, but in general Islam is not doloristic. I don't see Rumi disciplining himself harshly. The great saints certainly had an austere life, but they did not seek suffering. One of them loved to eat dates and deprived himself of them all his life. One day another saint, who was a friend of his, told him, "You would have done better to eat dates than to

---

4. One who experiences connection to the Divine using physical pain to imitate the suffering of Christ.

tell yourself all your life, 'My God, I have to avoid eating dates.'"

Loving the things of this life is not the greatest sin in Islam. No, the sin of all sins, to take the beautiful expression of Mounier,[5] is "the greed of the soul."

---

5. Emmanuel Mounier (1905–1950). French author and philosopher.

The event is all the more impressive because everyone is dressed the same. In effect, you are purified by ritual ablutions and then put on ihram, which means white clothing, also symbolizing purification. The purpose of this uniformity is also to eradicate differences. In Mecca, during the Hajj, officially there are no rich people, no poor people. There are only Muslims, all equal before their Lord.

XI

• **I'd like you to tell us about the pilgrimage to Mecca.**

I went two times, for the pilgrimage itself [*Hajj*][1] and for the simple visit [*'Umrah*].[2]

• **It must be rare for a Western woman to make the pilgrimage.**

It's not as exceptional as you think, but it is true that at that time it was more unusual.

• **The rule is that a Muslim must make the pilgrimage at least once in a lifetime.**

Yes, but on condition that it not be a hindrance for his family. You can't ruin yourself financially to go to Mecca, you can't deprive your dependents of their legitimate needs.

The date of the pilgrimage itself varies like the date for Easter varies for Christians [but moves over the entire year, because of the lunar calendar]. When it's in summer, it's obviously very hard because the heat is torrid. I made it in January and it was already terribly hot. There is also what is called the visit or the *'Umrah* (small pilgrimage), which can be made at any time of the year.

• **Non-Muslims don't have the right to go?**

It's been this way since the time of the Prophet. Probably out of fear of blind tourism or vandalism.

• **Once in a lifetime, that's not very often. How do you decide to go and why just at that particular time?**

The Hindus say, "When the disciple is ready, the spiritual guide

---

1. The *Hajj* is the annual pilgrimage which is obligatory for every able Muslim to perform once in his or her lifetime.
2. A visit anytime of the year to the sanctuary in Mecca is called an *'Umrah*, which includes specific rites.

appears." It's about the same thing for the pilgrimage. When the moment comes, you know. Something always happens to facilitate your departure.

I can tell you the story of one of my friends who is a lawyer in Fez. He decided to go in 1971 because his mother, who was already rather old, wanted at all costs to make the pilgrimage before dying. It was unfortunately a year when you could only take a very small amount of money out of Morocco. My friend was able to find foreign currency, but at the last minute, two days before leaving, he still needed a certain amount. Furious, on leaving his office, he got in his car and pulled out quickly. So quickly that he went down a one-way street. He was arrested by a policeman and, in taking out his papers from the glove compartment, he dropped an envelope. He opened it and realized that to the penny it contained the amount he needed. A little note from his secretary was attached to the money: "I don't know how to find you and I thought that you would surely open the glove compartment in your car, sooner or later. I was closing the office when a client arrived and said he remembered he owed you this amount."

You see, things like that always happen when you're leaving for the pilgrimage.

• **How did things go for you?**

I had wanted to make the pilgrimage for a long time, but a very good friend of mine kept repeating that I could not go alone. She had two cousins who were getting ready to leave but who didn't yet have permission. Because in Egypt, too, there were problems with foreign currency, so you had to ask permission from the municipal authorities. The authority was only granted to those who were going for the first time.

I didn't need authorization, but I made a misery of the lives of my friends by calling them constantly and I was disappointed to hear that the authorizations hadn't yet come through. One evening, I went to bed in a very bad mood and said to God, "Really, if I'm supposed to make this pilgrimage, do what is necessary." I went to sleep, and I saw in a dream a man that I didn't know at all. He was wearing an Egyptian robe with black and white stripes. He gave me a nice smile and said to me, "Welcome. You're going to leave for Medina."

I responded to him in a whining tone, "But I can't go to

Medina." He smiled at me again and said, "Yes, come to Medina." I was just asking myself what this meant when the telephone rang. It was the cousin of my friend. He said, "It's approved! We have the authorization. Run to the Saudi Arabian embassy to get your visa."

I jumped in a taxi. I arrived at the embassy, which is outside Cairo, and I saw at the door an immense Nubian, whom I asked where the office for the *Hajj* was. He said, "But you can't make the *Hajj*." I said that yes, I could, and he asked me if I were Turkish. I said that no, I wasn't, but that I still wanted to make the *Hajj* and he finally showed me the way.

I arrived and the ambassador's counselor, a very courteous man, took my papers and said, "Madame, I'm sorry. We have a new regulation. There are so many poor people who ask for a visa and later can't go because they don't have enough money that now we don't give a visa unless you have an airline ticket. Go quickly to United Arab Airlines, get your ticket, and I will be pleased to give you your visa."

I jumped back into the cab, ran to United Arab Airlines where they told me, "If you don't have your visa, we can't give you a ticket."

I turned around in this vicious circle for three days, after which, furious, I returned to the Saudi Arabian embassy. Alas, the gate was closed and there was a line a mile long of people waiting for it to open. I went straight to the gate and the immense Nubian, who recognized me, opened it slightly for me. I slipped in like a snake and went up to see the civil servant who had already received me. He welcomed me with a big smile and said, "Ah, madam, here's your passport with the visa. Congratulations. Pray for me during the *Hajj*." No doubt he had forgotten what he had told me the last time and I was careful not to remind him! I ran out like a thief, crossed the entire embassy, and came back panting to the back seat of my taxi.

I was bound for Mecca.

• **Was it at the time of the great pilgrimage?**

Yes, in January 1971. I swear that as soon as I arrived, I was stupefied to see such a crowd. I believe that we were more than two million people that year. The event is all the more impressive because everyone is dressed the same. In effect, you are purified by ritual ablutions and then put on *ihram*, which means white clothing, also symbolizing purification. The purpose of this uniformity is also to eradicate differences. In Mecca, during the *Hajj,* officially there are no rich people, no poor people. There are only Muslims, all equal before their Lord.

- **Do you really have the impression of being in a holy place?**

Absolutely. Don't forget that it was in Mecca, according to the tradition, that Abraham built the oldest standing temple to the one God. Abraham is supposed to have come there with his wife Haggar and his son Ishmael.

All the places recall history. You see the place where Haggar, dying of thirst, finally found water. Later, during the time of the pre-Islamic tribes, this place became a center for pagan idolatry. The Prophet Muhammad, who, you know, was originally from Mecca, made it the center of the new faith by purifying it of all idolatry and returning it to the worship of the one God.

If you will, Mecca represents for Muslims a little of what the Omphalos of Delphi[3] was for the Greeks, the center of the wheel toward which everything converges. It's like a vertical axis that draws people coming from all points of the world.

- **Did you circle the Kaaba?**

Naturally, seven times. It's the famous circumambulation. I can assure you that it's something to see this immense crowd turning slowly in place. I thought of Rilke: "All around my God, I turn throughout time."

- **What was for you the culminating moment of the pilgrimage?**

The last great assembly at Arafat, where you pray from sunrise to sunset. It's a great plain surrounded by hills. The hills are burnt sienna colored, but on that day they are so completely filled with people in white that the hills appear to be covered with snow.

---

3. The ancient Greeks considered Delphi to be the center of the world, and the stone Omphalos (literally the navel) of Delphi was the center of the universe. The famed oracle of Delphi, where rulers and beggars alike went to seek advice about the future, was in the same area. The Omphalos itself is a large decorated stone supported by three dancers, originally said to have been thrown by Zeus to identify the center of the world. Like Mecca, the Omphalos was the site of spiritual pilgrimages for contemplation and seeking wisdom or insight.

When the people leave, it's as if the snow is melting.

At the end of this last day, you buy a sheep to be sacrificed and the meat is given to the poor to eat.

I must admit that I didn't want to see a sheep slaughtered. During the war, I almost died of starvation in front of a chicken drinking in my kitchen because I just couldn't kill it. So you can imagine that a sheep was out of the question.

I accomplished the rites preceding the sacrifice, recreating symbolically the path that Haggar had followed while looking for water. You do this path seven times. I was barefoot, believing that it was required, and in the crowd an immense African pilgrim stepped on my toe, which hurt terribly. I almost passed out. They wanted me to go to the hospital, but I refused. They put a big bandage on it and gave me antibiotics and told me not to walk.

So that's why I didn't go see my sheep slaughtered. I was delighted, but the only problem was I had a problem with my foot for a long time. Years later, I sometimes still suffered from it.

- **Did you go to Medina?**

That's the second part of the pilgrimage. I really loved Medina which, as I said, reminded me a lot of Konya and Assisi.

There I was in the mosque. I wanted to approach the tomb of the Prophet, not to pray, because you don't pray to him, but still to see it from as close as possible. There was a surly fellow who, with the help of a big stick, stopped people from coming too close. When he was going to make us move, my friend, an Egyptian woman doctor, said to him, "Let her through, she's French." I saw the features of the guardian convulsing in horror, "A French woman on the *Hajj!*" he cried. I looked him right in the eye and recited in Arabic the prayer for the Prophet, "O Lord, bless your Prophet . . ." He immediately dropped his stick and took me by the hand, pressed me against the tomb and let me stay as long as I wanted.

- **You see, the man you dreamed about was right to say you were going to go to Medina.**

You don't know how right you are, because something else astonishing happened in this regard.

This man that I saw in my dream was a very ordinary looking gentleman, short, with a grey beard. I completed the pilgrimage and had forgotten about him. A few years later, in Egypt, I had been in close contact with an older sheikh who was half blind. When he had an operation for cataracts, I made the trip from Paris just to be near him. As he came out from the anesthesia, he said to me, "Finally, my dear, I will be able to see you."

When I returned to Cairo, I often went to his Sufi meeting place. One day, I realized that there was a painting on the wall so dusty that I had never noticed it before. A disciple there who, like me, was also a professor at al-Azhar, asked the sheikh about the picture. The sheikh had it brought to him, blew off the dust, and for a minute, my heart stopped beating. It was the portrait of the man that I had seen in my dream, with the exact same features.

The disciple asked the sheikh who it was and he replied, "A very nice man, the guardian of the mosque in Medina. He died ten years ago."

He would have just died when he appeared to me in the dream.

- **Hence the importance of remembering your dreams.**

This one, yes. You know there are two sorts of dreams, those that seem quite bizarre, and those that seem to come from afar.

- **I would like you to add a few words, to speak to us about the inner journey that the pilgrimage represents. How did you experience it and what did it bring you?**

You have probably noticed that I don't like to talk about my deep personal feelings. What I can nonetheless tell you is that I had the feeling of an extraordinary communion, a feeling of being a cell in an immense body, a bee in the hive, a corpuscle in the bloodstream. It's certainly a stunning moment of awareness. The palpable sense of a great brotherhood and sisterhood of millions of men and women, all praying the same way, turned in the same direction. A bit like what you sense when you fast during Ramadan, but even stronger.

- **The Islam that you love?**

Yes. I've tried to talk with you a little bit about Islam as I understand it, as it is lived by people such as Sheikh Bentounes and my Sufi friends, and all who have a certain openness of mind and of heart. That is what it means to be a Muslim: to have the feeling of belonging to a physical and mystical community.

Translator's Note:
How Paths Intertwine

Who is Eva de Vitray-Meyerovitch? With over forty publications, she is well-known in French-speaking countries. The entire world, however, deserves to know more about her. Although we can never completely know who another person is, this book tells the amazing tale of the woman who devoted so much of her life to translating the work of others.

In 1995, I was observing the first anniversary of my husband's death, and had spent a few days with French friends near Tours. We stopped in a small bookstore as I prepared to take the train back to Paris. My eyes lit on a title, *Anthology of Sufism* (in French *Anthologie du Soufisme*). I had become a voracious reader of books on Sufism, the mystical dimension, or aspect, of Islam.

After devouring the text, I knew this odd name of the author would be easy to find in a phone book. Indeed there it was, and I rang the number. Eva, I was told, was not well, but I could call back later in the day and speak with her. We spoke in French, although she had fluent English. She was happy to hear from a reader, and we engaged in one of those wonderfully wide-ranging discussions that glided from mysticism and grief, to countries, places and poets we loved.

Later, I mentioned our conversation to a French Jewish friend who was intrigued by Eva's life journey. When that friend came to visit me in the United States, she brought me another book by Eva, *Islam, l'autre visage*. While anthologies of Sufism exist in English, this text touched me because it revealed the personal side of a woman's voyage to which I could relate, the path to an awareness that passes only through the heart.

On my next trip to Paris, I called her and suggested this book really needed to be made available in English. She responded by asking me to come by for tea. I was thrilled, and made my way to her home in the Latin Quarter.

Aisha, who looked after Eva, welcomed me and showed me to the room where Eva sat upright in bed to receive guests. Eva apologized profusely for receiving me in her dressing gown, and I protested that, on the contrary, I was honored to be invited to visit. Eva was petite, even before she was bed-ridden, and although over 80 at the time, had startlingly fresh, wrinkle-free, lustrous skin.

She moved freely among multiple subjects, as she had in our telephone conversation, never once alluding to the book. After more than an hour, perhaps two, Eva paused and said, "I would like you to translate my book into English, please."

"But I am not a translator," I protested, "I'm an economist."

"No, but you understand and care about what I was saying, your French is beautiful, and English is your native language," she said.

Eva, a translator herself, knew far better than I what was involved the day she asked me to translate this small volume. As I was leaving, Aisha, brought me a book on Sufism by Sheikh Khaled Bentounes. She said I could borrow it and bring it back the next time I was in France.

"Now there is a sheikh worth meeting!" Eva said, and then added with a wink, "You know, he's quite a champion for women's rights."

In between my normal consulting on economic development projects, I began translating. In the process of shuffling words around, one undergoes a transformation, stepping into another person's world, for whatever interval. Eva did precisely this, imagining herself to be the disciple of her beloved Rumi for most of her adult life. Deciding to translate voluminous writings is not a task for one who enjoys public acclaim, because it involves iron discipline and a retreat from the world. She lived to fulfill this spiritual passion.

In the meantime, an American friend from one of Rumi's Mevlevi Sufi orders told me to contact a woman named Gray Henry. I didn't really know who she was, but was told she was an American who spent every December in Egypt. When we met, she said she was involved in publishing. I sensed that destiny was at work. I had the manuscript of the translation of Eva's book, but I hadn't even thought of a publisher yet. Would it be through Gray?

"You know, I have a manuscript, but I don't know anything about publishing," I said rather timidly.

"Really? Well, we work in a very specialized area so I'm probably not your publisher," she declared, and then added casually, "What's your text about, anyway?"

"It's a sort of biography about a French woman scholar of mysticism that I translated."

Gray's blue eyes opened wide in amazement, "Eva!" she exclaimed,

"The book is by Eva!"

"Why yes, it is, Eva de Vitray-Meyerovitch. How on earth did you know?"

"Eva visited us frequently when she was teaching at al-Azhar. You must show me the manuscript right away!"

When we met again, I showed her the text. The next time I saw her, she was as categorical as before.

"I must publish this book!" she said.

Eva was thrilled that I had been led to Gray in Egypt, yet not surprised at the workings of the Divine. That year, I visited Gray at her home in Kentucky. She was in the process of publishing a book about Thomas Merton's connection with Sufism. The American Trappist monk and mystic had been in contact with, and received a visit from, someone in Morocco named Sidi Abdessalam. She had copies of their correspondence and recordings of Merton describing the spiritual master's question to the Gethsemani monks. "Well brothers, are you getting what you came in here for?" She asked me if I could reach a certain sheikh from the central branch of the Shadhiliya Alawiya Sufi order in Algeria frequented by Sidi Abdessalam, when I next returned to France.

"Perhaps," mused Gray, "he might be able to shed some light on who Abdessalam was. The sheikh's name is Khaled Bentounes."

This was the very person Eva had insisted I contact! Suddenly I was no longer looking for *my* guide, but helping a friend gather information for *her* book!

Even now, over a decade after our first meeting and over twenty years since her own death, I feel Eva's presence as I recall the words of Rumi:

> When I die, do not look for me in the grave
> Seek me in the hearts of those whose lives I touched.

May the story of her life touch the minds of many readers and may the words of Rumi give our hearts wings.

Many thanks to Abdul Wadud Hughes and Dominique Krayenbuhl for their valuable contributions, as well as to Aisha, Eva's beloved caretaker, and Ingrid Jeffers.

This translation is dedicated to Tahar, without whom it would not have come into being.

Cathryn Goddard
Cairo, Egypt

Esin Çelebi, the twenty-second great granddaughter of Rumi,
in her office in Konya

Ms. Eva:
A Remembrance by Esin Çelebi

Ms. Eva was a scientist who was deeply respected by my father. She came to our house whenever she visited Istanbul. I met with her one-on-one and served her tea and coffee.

As you know, Ms. Eva became a Muslim, taking the name of Hawa. Her request in her will was: "Bury me in Hz. Mevlana's shadow." I heard of her will when I was very young. When she passed away in France after many years, her students reminded her sons of the request in her will. Her sons, with the new pain of loss, did not want to send their beloved mother to Turkey, to Konya. They did not want her grave be so far away, so they buried her at a place close to them.

After her death, her students started a foundation to continue her work and her legacy. They respected Ms. Eva's will, and researched it with care. As they worked one day at the Foundation, someone brought in a cassette tape of a speech given by Ms. Eva at a conference. She expressed her death wish in her own voice: "Bury me in Hz. Mevlana's shadow." After finding this tape, the students went to her children and let them hear it. Nine years had passed since Ms. Eva's death, and the pain had subsided for her sons, so they accepted the moving of the grave. According to the French law, a grave can be moved only during a ten-year period after the death; after this, it is not allowed. Before the expiration of the ten-year limit, the necessary paperwork was completed between the French and the Turkish governments.

Ten years after her death, Ms. Eva's grave was moved to the Üçler Cemetery in Konya [a burial grounds established in 1273, the year of Mevlana's death, which contains the original three (üç) graves of the Uçler family] next to Hz. Mevlana's tomb. A ceremony for Eva was held on December 17, the anniversary of Hz. Mevlana's death, which is known as the "Şeb-i Aruz." In this ceremony, the Governor of Konya, the Mayor of Konya and several Congressmen were present.

I also was able to attend this ceremony. People from many different countries were present. They had come to Konya for the "Şeb-i Aruz," and when they learned about the ceremony that was going to take place for Ms. Eva, they came. We can say that they came in response to Ms. Eva's spiritual invitation.

As I was watching the ceremony from some distance, I noticed Ismail Hoca, a Turkish *Hafiz* [a person who has learned to recite the Qur'an by heart] who lives in New York. He wanted to read something, but the other *Hafiz* present did not allow him to speak because they did not want to interrupt their program. I was saddened, and turned to an old journalist friend of mine and asked him to relay this message to Ismail Hoca: "Esin Çelebi is here. Please do not leave the ceremony. At the end, after everyone has gone, let's read a prayer together."

Ismail Hoca became very happy upon hearing this news. In fact, even though he was blind, he started to look around just as if he were seeing. When the ceremony was over and the crowd dispersed, a small group was left. We gathered in that small group at the grave – people from many different countries: the United States, Spain, France and even a lady from Lebanon. Then, I requested *Hafiz* Ismail to recite a beautiful section from the Qur'an. After that, according to the Mevlevi tradition, we repeated the name of God "Allah" many times at the grave. Professor Ibrahim Feracace from the US, who was standing next to me, asked, "With your permission, I would like to read a prayer in English." He read a prayer in English. Then, a Spanish lady who was standing next to Mr. Feracace sang a hymn in Spanish. The French person said, "I would like to read something in French." And so, there at the head of Ms. Eva's grave, many prayers were read in many languages. At the end, I read a Mevlevi prayer. This was a ceremony without preparation, coming directly from the heart.

There is a beautiful lesson we can learn from this story. I tell it to many young people as an example. Even after walking to the Truth (i.e., after death), a person can still receive gifts. Ms. Eva spent a lifetime in beautiful service and her wish came true ten years after her death.

Esin Çelebi
Istanbul, Turkey

Esin Çelebi Bayru is Vice President of the International Mevlana Foundation. She is Mevlana Jalaluddin Rumi's granddaughter from the 22nd generation, a descendent of Sultan Veled and Ulu Arif Çelebi.

Ten years after her death, Ms. Eva's grave was moved to the Üçler Cemetery in Konya ... next to Hz. Mevlana's tomb. A ceremony for Eva was held on December 17, the anniversary of Hz. Mevlana's death ... In this ceremony, the Governor of Konya, the Mayor of Konya and several Congressmen were present ... When the ceremony was over and the crowd dispersed, a small group was left. We gathered in that small group at the grave – people from many different countries. Among those present were Ibrahim Farajaje, Uzeyir Ozyurt, and Ismail Hoca.

While I was in Konya, I visited Sayeda Esin Çelebi, the 22nd great granddaughter of Rumi. I had known that she had been instrumental in bringing Eva's body to be reinterred in sight of Rumi's tomb, as had been Eva's wish.

Afterword:
From the Publisher

This wonderful volume came as a great gift to me, in that it completed a most blessed friendship with dear Eva. It introduced me to many dimensions of her thought and life of which I was unaware during our years of friendship in both Cairo and Paris. I can *literally* hear the voice of Eva in this translated series of interviews – almost as though our conversation was simply picked up again and had hardly ever been interrupted.

I can picture Eva sitting in our living room in Cairo, with her pale red hair drawn up in a bun, knitting and nibbling on a few chocolates. Each evening, she would read from her Rumi translations to my husband Fyodor. It was noted that a tiny spider would crawl out and sit on the arm of the great green couch in front of the fireplace to listen as well. At the end of the reading, the precious spider would withdraw, awaiting the next session. Fyodor mentioned that as Eva read the lines "Me" "You" and "I," one became confused as to Who one really is/was.

In July of 1973, I attended the inauguration of a beautiful mosque built in the cemetery high up below the Muqqattam Hills, from which the Pyramids could be seen in the far distance beyond the Nile. The backstory of the mosque's creation provides one more link to Eva. The burial place of the great saint, Ibn 'Ata' Allah al-Iskandari (d. 1309), had been lost. The Rector of al-Azhar University and *Sheikh al-Islam,* Sheikh Abd al-Haleem Mahmoud (whose doctoral work was completed at the Sorbonne), asked a friend of ours and some others to try to locate the site where Ibn 'Ata' Allah had been buried so that the place could be properly marked and acknowledged. This company of friends set about digging in the appropriate vicinity, near to the shrine of Ali al-Wafa, who followed in the spiritual lineage of Ibn 'Ata' Allah. Suddenly there arose from the excavation area the smell of perfume – which was described by those digging as a "perfume not of this world," but paradisal. Soon they came upon the actual body of Ibn 'Ata'

Allah, which had remained unchanged. The bodies of some saints do not seem to be subject to time or decay, but remain as they were before death.

Over this hallowed spot a small prayer room was constructed, which included a *mushrabiyaa* (wooden lattice) screen surrounding the cenotaph indicating the place of burial below. In this chamber hangs a wonderful photograph of Sheikh Abdul Haleem next to the grave of Sheikh Abu al-Hasan al-Shadhili. Later it was decided that a mosque should be built and attached to this small shrine. The patron, who saw to the finances of this undertaking, noticed that each time he went to remove needed funds from his safe, the original amount miraculously never diminished. Surprised, he mentioned this to Sheikh Abd al-Haleem, who then explained that if he mentioned this occurrence to anyone, the funds would begin to deplete when drawn upon.

When the beautiful mosque, decorated with geometric designs painted on the ceiling, was completed, many friends assembled for the inauguration. Sheikh Abd al-Haleem climbed up the *minbar* (pulpit) and spoke. Among those present was, of course, his friend Hawa (Eva) de Vitray-Meyerovitch who was preparing to make the Hajj. I remember thinking on this occasion that I was present to a truly angelic assembly of souls – a kind of preview of the Next Realm.

Around that time, a friend of Eva's from Paris arrived to join her on her upcoming pilgrimage. Taharah had been a Carmelite nun in Paris who was entrusted with certain privileges outside of the convent, which included caring for the financial matters of her order. One day, as she passed along the street, she overheard the words of Eva who was lecturing about Islam. Taharah ended up converting to Islam as well, and here she was, having tea in our home in Maadi.

I hadn't realized until reading these interviews with Eva that she had studied Sanskrit. Suddenly, I understood why she had wanted to have morning coffee at the nearby home of Moyyiene al-Arab. Sophia, his English wife, served us in her wondrous English garden, complete with cockatoos, horses, and her famous parrot, Bin Bin. Moyyiene was a Vedantist with more than a great interest in Hindu metaphysics. I will never forget his opening remarks to Eva as he appeared in his beautiful white suit and hat, "If we are not here to discuss Ultimate Truth and the underlying principles of Reality, we may as well disband."

In his Introduction to this book, Sheikh Khaled Bentounes mentions a visit of Eva to the *zawiyya* of Sheikh Hafiz Tijani. When she asked to become his disciple, he merely put his mantle around her shoulders and mentioned that he could not take her on because he would give her so many prayers and recitations to say each day that he worried she would become guilty from being unable to keep up. I was present for this exchange, and thought a further description of the setting would be of interest. Sheikh Hafiz Tijani had become blind but could *see*. Four or five of us, two from Japan, sat with him around a small low table on which was set a bowl of stew. Pieces of the wonderful Egyptian brown bran bread were placed around the bowl, serving as utensils. Just before lunch concluded, an eye doctor from Shemeen al-Kom appeared. The name of Sheikh Hafiz Tijani referred to the fact he was a renowned *hafiz* (he who had memorized) of hadith. The doctor wanted to know if there were any references in all of the hadith collections (of which there are volumes) to a certain plant which he thought might be useful as a cure for eye diseases. Eva's mouth dropped open when Sheikh Hafiz Tijani responded: "In my humble knowledge of hadith, there are only three references to this plant." He proceeded to recite two of these, including the entire *isnad,* or chain of transmission going back to the Prophet Muhammad, for each one of the prophetic traditions which referred to the plant. He then said, "However, I am unsure about the *isnad* of the third one." He called over a young boy who assisted him and asked that he climb up to a long bookshelf above a wall of closets and bring down the third volume from the left. We all covered our faces as he dusted off this book. Sheikh Hafiz Tijani then said, "Open the book to around the middle and read," after which he instructed the boy to go back two pages and read the hadith to be found at the bottom. And there it was.

The last time we saw Eva was in the 1980s, when we came over with our children from Cambridge to visit her in her apartment on the rue Claude Bernard in Paris, but in a way I got to see her again just a couple of years ago. While I was in Konya, I visited Sayeda Esin Çelebi, the 22nd great granddaughter of Rumi. I had known that she had been instrumental in bringing Eva's body to be reinterred in sight of Rumi's tomb, as had been Eva's wish. You will have read about this in Madame Esin's essay, included above.

When we visited Eva's grave, there was a cat snuggled up against it, warming itself in the sun. I remembered how much Eva adored cats and how much they were drawn to her! I greeted her, "Peace and blessings be upon you, Blessed Friend Eva, I love you."

Gray Henry
Louisville, Kentucky
July, 2020

Emine Dilşda Çavuş and Esin Çelebi

Bibliography of Works
by Eva de Vitray-Meyerovitch*

1935. Li Chang. *Mœurs des mandarins sous la dynastie mandchoue.* Translated from th–e English. Paris: Payot, 1935.

1955. Iqbal, Mohammed. *Reconstruire la pensée religieuse de l'Islam.* Translated from the original English and notes by Eva de Vitray-Meyerovitch. Preface by Louis Massignon. Paris: Librairie d'Amérique et d'Orient, 1955; Adrien-Maisonneuve, 1995; Monaco: Rocher, 1996.

1956. Fryzee, Asaf Ali Adghar. *Conférences sur l'Islam.* Translation by Eva de Vitray-Meyerovitch, preface by Louis Massignon. Paris: CNRS, 1956.

1956. Iqbal, Mohammed. *Message de l'Orient.* Translated from the original English by Eva de Vitray-Meyerovitch and Mohammad Achena. Paris: Société d'Edition les Belles Lettres, 1956.

1962. Iqbal, Mohammed. *Le livre de l'éternité.* Translated from the original English by Eva de Vitray-Meyerovitch, avec la collaboration de Mohammed Mokri. Paris: Albin Michel, 1962.

1964. Vitray-Meyerovitch, Eva de. *Henri VIII.* Paris: Julliard, 1964, 1972.

1968. Rees, Richard, *Simone Weil: esquisse d'un portrait.* Translated from the English by Eva de Vitray-Meyerovitch. Paris: Buchet-Chastel, 1968.

1968. Vitray-Meyerovitch, Eva de. *Thèmes mystiques dans l'œuvre de Djalal-ud-din Rumi.* Doctoral dissertation, 1968.

1972. Vitray-Meyerovitch, Eva de. *Mystique et poésie en Islam: Djalal-ud-Din Rumi et l'ordre des derviches tourneurs.* Paris: Desclée de Brouwer, 1972, 1982.

1973. Jalal-al-din Rumi Maulana. *Odes mystiques.* Translated from the Persian by Eva de Vitray-Meyerovitch and Mohammad Mokri. Paris: Klincksieck, 1973, 1984; Paris: Seuil, 2003.

---

* Bibliography from *Ink of Light,* by Katharine Branning, Fons Vitae 2018, a double biographical novel depicting the intertwined paths of Rumi and Eva de Vitray-Meyerovitch in a dialog across time.

1974. Zaehner, R.C. *L'Hindouisme*. Translated from the original English by Eva de Vitray-Meyerovitch. Paris: Desclée De Brouwer, 1974.

1976. Attar, Farid al-Din. *Le mémorial des saints (Taz'Kerrat al-awliya)*. Translated from the Ouigour by A. Pavet de Courteille. Preface by Eva de Vitray-Meyerovitch. Paris: Le Seuil, 1976.

1976. Jalal-al-din Rumi Maulana. *Le livre du dedans: fihi-ma-fihi*. Translated from the Persian by Eva de Vitray-Meyerovitch. Paris: Sinbad, 1976, 1989; Paris: Albin Michel, 1997; Arles: Actes Sud, 2010. Translated into Italian and Spanish.

1977. Vitray-Meyerovitch, Eva de. *Rumi et le Soufisme*. Paris: Seuil, 1977, 2001, 2005, 2015. Translated into English, Roumanian, Portuguese, Bosnian, and Czech.

1978. Vitray-Meyerovitch, Eva de. *Anthologie du soufisme*. Paris: Sinbad, 1978, 1986, 1989; Albin Michel, 1995.

1978. Vitray-Meyerovitch, Eva de. *Approche symbolique de l'écriture chez quelques mystiques musulmans*. Tunis: Université de Tunis, [1978].

1982. Vitray-Meyerovitch, Eva de. *Les Chemins de la lumière: 75 contes soufis*. Paris: Retz, 1982. Translated into Spanish.

1982. Sultan Valad. *Maître et disciple*. Translated from the original Persian by Djamchid Mortazavi and Eva de Vitray-Meyerovitch. Paris: Sinbad, 1982.

1983. Zaehner, R.C. *Mystique sacrée, mystique profane*. Translated from the original English by Eva de Vitray-Meyerovitch. Monaco: Editions du Rocher, 1983.

1984. Hirashima, Hussein Yoshio et Eva de Vitray-Meyerovitch. *La Mecque: ville sainte de l'Islam*. Paris: R. Laffont, 1984.

1984. Vitray-Meyerovitch, Eva de. *Islam, Christianisme*. Saint-Zacharie (France): Editions de l'Ouvert, 1984.

1984. Vitray-Meyerovitch, Eva de. *La Mecque: ville sainte de l'Islam*. Paris: R. Laffont, 1984. Translated into Italian, German, and Turkish.

1984. Vitray-Meyerovitch, Eva de, André Borrély, and Jean-Yves Leloup. *L'image de l'homme dans le Christianisme et l'Islam*. [Saint-Zacharie, France]: Editions de l'Ouvert, 1984.

1987. Jalal-al-din Rumi Maulana. *Rubai'yat*. Translated from the original Persian by Eva de Vitray-Meyerovitch. Paris: Albin Michel, 1987, 1993, 2003.

1988. Mortazavi, Djamchid. *Le Secret de l'unité dans l'estorisme iranien*.

Preface de Eva de Vitray-Meyerovitch. Paris: Dervey, 1988.

1988. Vitray-Meyerovitch, Eva de. *Présence de l'Islam*. Konya: Selçuk Universitesi, 1988.

1988. Sultan Valad. *La Parole secrète: enseignement du maitre soufi Rumi*. Translated from the original Persian by Djamchid Mortazavi and Eva de Vitray-Meyerovitch. Monaco: Rocher, 1988.

1989. Iqbal, Mohammed. *Les secrets de soi, les mystères du non-moi*. Translated from the Persian by Djamchid Mortazavi and Eva de Vitray-Meyerovitch. Paris: Albin Michel, 1989.

1989. Vitray-Meyerovitch, Eva de. *Konya ou la danse cosmique*. Paris: Jacqueline Renard, 1989. Translated into Turkish.

1989. Vitray-Meyerovitch, Eva de, Marc-Alain Descamps, Marie-Madeleine Davy, and Jampa Tartchin. *L'amour transpersonnel*. Lavaur: Trismegiste, 1989.

1990. Jalal-al-din Rumi Maulana. *Lettres*. Translated from the Persian by Eva de Vitray-Meyerovitch. Paris: J. Renard, 1990.

1990. Jalal-al-din Rumi Maulana. *Mathnawi: la quête de l'absolu*. Translated from the original Persian by Eva de Vitray-Meyerovitch and Djamchid Mortazavi. Monaco: Rocher, 1990, 2013.

1991. Vitray-Meyerovitch, Eva de. *L'islam, l'autre visage*: entretiens avec Rachel et Jean-Pierre Cartier. Paris: Criterion, 1991; Albin Michel, 1995. Translated into Spanish, English, and Turkish.

1991. Shabistari, Mahmud ibn al-Karim. *La Roseraie du mystère*. Translated from the Persian with presentation and notes by Djamchid Mortazavi and Eva de Vitray-Meyerovitch. Paris: Sinbad, 1991; Arles: Actes Sud, 2013.

1992. Zaehner, R.C. *Inde, Israël, Islam: religions mystiques et révélations prophétiques*. Translated from the original English by Eva de Vitray-Meyerovitch. Paris: Desclée De Brouwer, 1992.

1993. Jalal-al-din Rumi Maulana. *Le Chant du Soleil*. Translations by Eva de Vitray-Meyerovitch and Marie-Pierre Chevrier. Paris: Table Ronde, 1993, 1997. Translated into Spanish and Turkish.

1995. Skali, Faouzi et Eva de Vitray-Meyerovitch. *Jésus dans la tradition soufie*. Le Plan-d'Aups: Ed. de l'Ouvert, 1995; Paris: Albin Michel Spiritualités, 2004, 2013. Translated in Italian, Spanish, and Catalan.

1996. Iqbal, Mohammed. *La métaphysique en Perse.* Translated from the original English by Eva de Vitray-Meyerovitch. Paris: Sinbad, 1980; Arles: Actes Sud, 1996.

1996. Iqbal, Mohammed. *Reconstruire la pensée religieuse de l'Islam.* Translated from the original English and notes by Eva de Vitray-Meyerovitch. Preface by Louis Massignon. Paris: Adrien-Maisonneuve, 1995; Monaco: Rocher, 1996.

1997. Vitray-Meyerovitch, Eva de. *La Prière en Islam.* With the collaboration of Tewfik Taleb. Paris: Grand Livre du mois, 1997; Albin Michel, 1997, 2003. Translated into Italian and Turkish.

2000. Jalal-al-din Rumi Maulana. *Les quatrains de Rumi.* Translated from the Persian by Eva de Vitray-Meyerovitch. Paris: Albin Michel, 2000.

2001. Gazali, Muhammad ibn Muhammad Abu Hamid al-. *Revivication des sciences de la religion and les secrets de la prière en Islam.* Translated by Eva de Vitray-Meyerovitch and Tewfik Taleb. Beyrouth: al-Bouraq, 2001.

2014. Vitray-Meyerovitch, Eva de. *Universalité de l'Islam.* Commentaires de Jean-Louis Girotto. Paris: Albin Michel, 2014. (Postmortem publication of various articles by Eva de Vitray-Meyerovitch.)